UNVEILING AUTISM

Exposing Mental imbalance and Investigating the New Essences of Neurodiversity

Fernanda D. Barr

Disclaimer Copyright © by Fernanda D. Barr 2023. All rights reserved.
Before this document is duplicated or reproduced in any manner, the publisher's consent must be gained. Therefore, the contents within can neither be stored electronically, transferred, nor kept in a database. Neither in Part nor full can the document be copied, scanned, faxed, or retained without approval from the publisher or creator

Unveiling Autism

Table of contents

Introduction

The most fundamental human activities provide difficulties for children with autism. They have trouble relating to others and frequently fail to recognize them as actual individuals and not just inanimate things. They find it difficult to express their thoughts and feelings, have a hard time picturing what other people are thinking or feeling, and in some cases go their entire lives without speaking. They usually struggle to connect with others, even their own family.

The best way to describe autism is as a spectrum of illnesses with varying symptom intensity, onset ages, and associations with other disorders (e.g., mental retardation, specific language delay, epilepsy). Over time, a child's autistic symptoms might change significantly both within and between individuals. Although there are clear and persistent similarities, particularly in terms of social deficiencies, there is no one behaviour that is always indicative of autism and no conduct that would automatically disqualify a particular kid from receiving a diagnosis of autism. Experienced clinicians and educators can easily and reliably identify the wide range of behaviours that define autistic spectrum disorders in very young children, which typically represent deficits in social interaction, verbal and nonverbal communication, and constrained patterns of interest or behaviour. Distinctions between classical autism and atypical autism, pervasive developmental disorder-not otherwise specified (PDD-NOS), and Asperger's disorder, however, can be arbitrary and are frequently connected with the presence or severity of disabilities, such as mental retardation and severe language impairment. For some research projects, it is necessary to classify autism into specific subgroups; nevertheless, it is debatable whether there are any therapeutic or educational advantages to categorising autistic spectrum disorders solely according to diagnosis. Individual variations in language development, verbal and nonverbal communication, motor or sensory skills, adaptive behaviour, and cognitive abilities, on the other hand, have a significant impact on behavioural presentation and outcome, and as a result, have particular implications for educational goals and strategies. Hence, the child's strengths and weaknesses, the age of diagnosis, and early intervention are the most crucial factors to take into account when programming. Several families claim that even earlier than this, they began to worry about their children's behaviour and expressed it, typically to health professionals. For even younger ages, research is being done to create trustworthy identification techniques. Children with autistic spectrum disorders, like kids with vision or hearing issues, need early identification and diagnosis to give them the skills (like imitation and communication) to benefit from educational services. There is some evidence to suggest that starting autistic spectrum disorder-specific services earlier is linked to a better response to treatment. Hence, well-intentioned attempts to avoid giving children official diagnoses can prevent them from receiving specialist care. Children as young as two years old should be identified as being on the autism spectrum at an early age for a variety of reasons. According to epidemiological research and service-based data, the prevalence of autism spectrum disorders has increased over the past ten years, in part because educators, doctors, and other professionals have become better at identifying and categorising these conditions. There is no denying that more kids are being recognized as having autism spectrum disorders and needing specialised educational interventions.

The main type of treatment for this enigmatic illness is education. This implies that we impose significant duties on the schools, teachers, parents, and other professionals who work with autistic children.

Chapter 1

Exploring Autism

Autism Spectrum Disorder is another name for autism (ASD). The term "spectrum" describes the diverse set of traits, aptitudes, and skills that individuals with autism have. Autism does not have the same effects on every single person. Every person with autism has a unique experience and requires a different level of support. Although the fundamental traits of autism can lead to a variety of difficulties, it's crucial to understand that they can also provide distinctive skills and abilities.

Although autism is a lifelong disorder, both children and adults with it can make considerable improvement and lead happy, fulfilled lives with the right care. Therefore, it is crucial that people with autism have access to specialised services that are knowledgeable about their requirements and skilled in fostering their abilities.

As a result, those who have autism are not alone. Furthermore, even if you don't have autism yourself, it's possible that you know someone who does.

At this moment, men are 3.5 times more likely than women to have autism.

The rise in prevalence rates does not necessarily indicate an increase in the incidence of autism. Instead, it's possible that more knowledge and understanding of autism, together with modifications to the diagnostic criteria, have improved the ability to recognize its symptoms.

A wide range of diseases collectively known as autism, or autistic spectrum disorder (ASD), is characterised by difficulties with social skills, repetitive activities, speech, and nonverbal communication. The Centers for Disease Control estimate that one in every 36 children in the United States currently suffers from autism.

We are aware that there are numerous subtypes of autism, the majority of which are driven by a confluence of hereditary and environmental variables. Since autism is a spectrum disorder, each autistic individual has a unique set of abilities and difficulties. People with autism can learn, reason, and solve problems in a variety of ways, from highly skilled to severely impaired. While some persons with ASD could need a lot of everyday assistance, others might only need a little help and in some circumstances could even live independently.

Many variables may impact the development of autism, and it is commonly accompanied by sensory sensitivity and physiological concerns such as gastrointestinal (GI) illnesses, seizures or sleep disorders, as well as mental health challenges such as anxiety, depression and attention issues.

Symptoms of autism commonly develop by age 2 or 3. Certainly linked development delays can emerge even sooner, and often, they can be detected as early as 18 months. Studies suggest that early intervention leads to favourable results later in life for people with autism.

In 2013, the American Psychiatric Association unified four separate autism diagnoses into one umbrella diagnosis of autism spectrum disorder (ASD) (ASD). These included autistic disorder, childhood disintegrative disorder, pervasive developmental disorder-not otherwise defined (PDD-NOS) and Asperger syndrome.

Early intervention can alter a life.

Studies have made evident that high-quality early intervention can increase learning, communication and social skills, as well as underlying brain development. Experts believe numerous origins of ASD act together to affect the most typical ways people develop. We still have much to learn about these reasons and how they affect people with ASD.

People with ASD might act, impart, draw in, and advance in manners that are unique in relation to most others. There is commonly nothing about how they look that separates them from others. The gifts of individuals with ASD could contrast enormously. For instance, certain individuals with ASD might have progressed discourse capacities while others might be nonverbal. A few people with ASD need a great deal of help in their everyday existence; others can work and live with practically no help.

ASD starts at 3 years old and can endure all through an individual's life, despite the fact that side effects might work on over the long run. A few youngsters show ASD signs inside the initial year of life. In others, side effects may not appear until two years old enough or later. A few kids with ASD gain new abilities and arrive at formative objectives until around 18 to two years old enough, and afterward they quit growing new abilities or lose the gifts they previously had.

As kids with ASD arrive at teenagers and youthful grown-ups, they might experience difficulty making and keeping up with kinships, conversing with friends and grown-ups, or grasping what ways of behaving are expected in school or at work. They might come to the consideration of medical services specialists since they additionally have conditions like tension, gloom, or consideration shortfall/hyperactivity jumble, which happen more frequently in people with ASD than in individuals without ASD.

What Is the Mental imbalance Range Problem?

Mental imbalance range jumble (ASD) is a convoluted formative sickness with constant issues with social correspondence, confined interests, and tedious way of behaving. While mental imbalance is viewed as a long lasting disease, the level of hindrance in working in light of these issues varies among people with mental imbalance.

Analyse of Mental imbalance Range Issues

Early signs of this sickness can be seen by guardians/parental figures or paediatricians before a kid arrives at one year old enough. However, side effects frequently become all the more consistently observable when a youngster is 2 or 3 years of age. In specific conditions, the utilitarian impedance because of mental imbalance might be moderate and not clear until the youngster goes to class, after which their lacks might be articulated while among their cohorts.

Social correspondence troubles may include1:

•Diminished sharing of interests with others

•Difficulty appreciating their own and others' feelings
•Abhorrence for keeping in touch
•Absence of capability with the utilisation of non-verbal signals
•Unnatural or prearranged discourse
•Taking unique ideas in a real sense
•Troubles making companions or holding them
Restricted interests and monotonous ways of behaving may include1:
•The firmness of lead, incredible trouble adapting to change
•Being too focused on specialty issues to the rejection
•Anticipating that others should be similarly keen on those things
•Inconvenience tolerating changes in daily practice and new encounters
•Tactile excessive touchiness
•Cliché activities, for example, hand fluttering, shaking, turning
•Putting things, particularly toys, in an extremely specific way
•Parent/guardian/educator worries about the youngster's direct ought to prompt a particular assessment by a formative paediatrician, paediatric clinician, kid nervous system specialist or potentially a kid and juvenile therapist. This assessment

involves scrutinising the parent/guardian, noticing, and efficiently collaborating with the youngster, and incidentally finishing extra tests to preclude different issues. In a few confounding conditions, the finding of chemical imbalance might be conceded, however generally, an early determination can significantly further develop a youngster's work by giving the family early admittance to supporting assets locally.

Most parents start with their paediatrician who is checking on developmental milestones. If your child is under the age of 3 years, you can seek an evaluation through your local early intervention system. If your child is over the age of 3, you can get an evaluation through your local school (even if your child does not go there) (even if your child does not go there). Call your local school's preschool special education team to seek an evaluation.

The current knowledge reveals that various genetic variables may enhance the chance of autism in a complex manner. Possessing certain specific genetic disorders such as Fragile X Syndrome and Tuberous Sclerosis has been recognized as providing a substantially higher risk for being diagnosed with autism. Some drugs, such as valproic acid and thalidomide, when used during pregnancy, have been connected with an increased risk of autism as well. Having a sibling with autism also raises the probability of a child being diagnosed with autism. Parents being older at the time of pregnancy is additionally connected with the increasing risk of autism. Vaccines on the other hand have not been demonstrated to raise the likelihood of an autism diagnosis, and race, ethnicity or socioeconomic background does not seem to have a link either. Male children tend to be diagnosed with autism more often than those assigned female sex at birth, albeit this ratio is shifting with time.

ASD comprises numerous conditions within the spectrum. ASD alters the way your child interacts and communicates. There's no cure for autism, but the symptoms may reduce over time.

Autism, often named autism spectrum disorder (ASD), is a neurodevelopmental condition. ASD is a developmental impairment caused by variations in your child's brain. Individuals with ASD may behave, engage and learn in ways that are different from other people. They may have problems with social relations and with comprehending and using nonverbal and vocal communication.

Problems communicating with other individuals or variances in how they engage with others.

•Difficulty using and interpreting nonverbal communication, like eye contact, facial expressions.

•Late language progress.

•Difficulty creating and comprehending connections.

•Repeated motor actions, including flapping arms, body shaking or repetitious speaking or play.

•Insistence on sameness in environment or habit.

•Strong or unique interests.

•Sensory aversions, such as hatred of loud noises, or sensory-seeking behaviours.

ASD varies greatly in severity and everyday impairment, the symptoms of certain persons aren't always immediately recognized

Forms of Autism Spectrum Disorders

There are three categories of autism spectrum disorders:

Autistic Disorder

This is frequently dubbed "classic" autism. That is what most people think of when hearing the phrase "autism". Individuals with autism disorder frequently have major language deficits, social and communication issues, and unique habits and interests. Many people with autism also have an intellectual handicap.

Asperger Syndrome

Individuals with Asperger syndrome usually have milder symptoms of autistic disorder. They could have social issues and unique actions and hobbies. Yet, they often do not have problems with language or intellectual disabilities.

Atypical Autism

This is sometimes dubbed "atypical autism," or PDD-NOS. Individuals who fit some of the criteria for autistic disorder or Asperger syndrome, but not all, may be diagnosed with atypical autism. These persons normally have fewer and milder symptoms than those with autism disorder. The symptoms could cause only social and communication issues. The findings of this research reveal a substantial component in the underlying causes of neural tube birth abnormalities, intellectual impairments, and autism risk.

Researchers from Texas A&M College of Medicine have revealed answers to crucial issues concerning how the neocortex develops, revealing fresh information regarding the core causes of intellectual disorders.

A substantial improvement in our understanding of how the brain grows has been reached by researchers at Texas A&M University College of Medicine. This new research increases our understanding of how the part of the brain that distinguishes humans from other animals develops and gives light on what causes intellectual difficulties, such as autism spectrum disorders.

For many years, scientists have identified a substantial association between mammalian intelligence and a thin layer of cells in the neocortex, the part of the brain that governs higher-order activities like cognition, perception, and languages .The neocortex's surface region reflects how exceptionally fostered a life form's psychological capacity is. For instance, the human neocortex is only roughly three times thicker than the mouse equivalent. Yet, the human neocortex has a 1,000-fold higher surface area than that of mice. Autism spectrum disorders and intellectual disabilities are among the developmental defects induced by abnormalities in this region of the brain.

What is unknown is how evolutionary expansion of this portion of the brain happens selectively in favour of enlarging the neocortex's surface area at the cost of increasing its thickness. A crucial component of this process is how the early populations of neural stem cells, which act as the brain's building blocks, disseminate themselves.

"There are many, what we'll call, separate handling units that are on a level plane situated in the neocortex.

The more surface region you have, the greater number of these handling units you can oblige," said Vytas A. Bankaitis, Recognized Teacher at the School of Medication, E.L. Wehner-Welch Establishment Seat in Science, and co-creator of this review, which was distributed in Cell Reports. "The inquiry is, the reason is the neocortical surface region is so much higher compared with its thickness as one ascends the mammalian transformative tree? For what reason do cerebrum undifferentiated cells along the side convey themselves as they develop and not heap on top of another?"

This point is huge on the grounds that when the cells don't fan out, yet rather stack up, it creates a denser neocortex with a more modest surface region - a characteristic that has been distinguished in instances of scholarly hindrance and even chemical imbalance.

"One of the most explored hereditary explanations behind scholarly handicap is a change in a quality that was previously assigned LIS1," said Zhigang Xie, partner teacher at the Staff of Medication and co-creator of the review. "This hereditary transformation will create a smooth cerebrum, which is associated with scholarly hindrance. Also, one common perception is that the neocortex of the patient is thicker than typical. There are additionally genuinely new examinations that demonstrate normal attributes in the mind of chemical imbalance that remember strangely thickened locales of the neocortex for those people."

Researchers have referred to for quite a while that as brain foundational microorganisms partition, their cores relocate all over inside their physical space as a result of the phone cycle, a peculiarity called interkinetic atomic movement. They do as such by utilising a cytoskeletal network that behaves like train follows motors that move the cores up or down in a firmly controlled way. Albeit a few thoughts have been proposed, it remains a conundrum why the cores move along these lines, how this organisation of train tracks is controlled, and which job interkinetic atomic relocation plays in the improvement of the neocortex.

Concerning why, Bankaitis makes sense that when there are such countless cells so near one another in the undeveloped phase of neocortical turn of events, the development of their cores all over causes restricting vertical and descending powers that spread the isolating brain immature microorganisms out.

"Ponder a container of toothpaste," Bankaitis said. "If you somehow managed to take that toothpaste tube, put it between your hands, push up from the base and push down from the top, what might occur? It would straighten and fan out. That is basically how this functions. You have a vertical power and a descending power made by the development of the core that spreads these cells out."

Xie and Bankaitis additionally uncover how the cells do this by consolidating many separate pathways that coordinate to "tell" the infant brain immature microorganisms where to go.

"I think interestingly, this genuinely arranges atoms and flagging pathways that uncover how this cycle is overseen and why it would be associated or connected with neurodevelopmental lacks," Bankaitis said. "They have taken a biochemical interaction, coupled it to a phone science pathway, and related it to a flagging pathway that discusses to the core to invigorate the atomic way of behaving that produces a power that fosters a modern mind. It's presently a total circuit."

The consequences of this study uncover a pivotal component in the fundamental reasons for mental imbalance risk, scholarly handicap and brain tube birth irregularities. The new comprehension of the essential standards deciding the construction of the neocortex will likewise empower the plan of in vitro mind culture frameworks that all the more exactly emulate the formative cycles of interest and increment the opportunities for neurological medication advancement.

"While there could be different justifications for why a neocortex thickens as opposed to spreading, our work gives another perspective on why patients with chemical imbalance and scholarly hardships by and large present a thicker cortex," Xie said. "The way that the LIS1 quality item is an essential controller of atomic relocation, including the interkinetic atomic movement that they investigate in this work, supports the ends we make in this paper."

Chapter 2

Autism in young children

•Dodges or doesn't keep eye to eye connection

•Doesn't answer name by 9 months old enough

•Doesn't show looks like happy, miserable, angry, and stunned by 9 months old enough

•Could not play straightforward intelligent games at any point like pat-a-cake by a year old enough

•Utilises not many or no movements at a year old enough (for instance, doesn't say farewell) (for instance, doesn't say farewell)

•Doesn't impart interests to others by 15 months old enough (for instance, shows you an item that they like) (for instance, shows you an article that they like)

•Doesn't highlight show you something entrancing by year and a half old enough

•Doesn't see when others are harmed or unglued about two years old enough

•Doesn't see different kids and go along with them in play by three years old enough

•Doesn't claim to be something different, like an instructor or superhuman, during play by four years old enough

•Doesn't sing, dance, or represent you by 60 months old enough

•Restricted or Rehashed Ways of behaving or Interests

People with ASD display activities or interests that can appear to be unusual. These ways of behaving or interests lay out ASD separated from messes depicted by trouble with social correspondence and association as it were.

Instances of confined or tedious propensities and interests related with ASD can incorporate

•Close-up of a kid playing with toy blocks on the floor covering

•Lines up toys or different things and gets despondent when request is upset

•Rehashes words or expressions again and again (called echolalia) (called echolalia)

•Plays with toys the same way like clockwork

Is centred around areas of things (for instance, wheels) (for instance, wheels)

•Gets disturbed by little changes

•Has urgent interests

•Should follow specific schedules

•Folds hands, rocks body, or twists self in circles\sHas odd responses to the manner in which things sound, smell, taste, look, or feel

•Different Characteristics

The vast majority with ASD have extra important highlights. They could incorporate

•Postponed language abilities

•Deferred development abilities

•Postponed mental or acquiring abilities

•Hyperactive, incautious, and additionally •negligent way of behaving

•Epilepsy or seizure problem

•Odd eating and dozing propensities

•Gastrointestinal issues (for instance, blockage) (for instance, stoppage)

•Uncommon state of mind or close to home responses
•Tension, stress, or unjustifiable concern
•Non Appearance of dread or more apprehension than anticipated
•It is essential to take note of that youngsters with ASD might not have all or a portion of the ways of behaving depicted as models here

Asperger disorder

Asperger versus mental imbalance - what's the distinction?

Medical care experts don't officially perceive Asperger disorder as its condition any longer. They used to think about Asperger's and chemical imbalance as unmistakable circumstances. The side effects that were initially essential for an Asperger's finding currently fall under the chemical imbalance range. Suppliers think about Asperger's, a gentle kind of mental imbalance. Certain individuals actually utilise the name Asperger's disorder to portray their condition.

Mental imbalance Range Issue Signs and Side effects

Mental imbalance range jumble (ASD) is a formative hindrance brought about by irregularities in the cerebrum. People with ASD by and large dislike social correspondence and cooperation, and restricted or dreary propensities or side interests. People with ASD may likewise have various approaches to getting the hang of, moving, or focusing. It is pivotal to take note of that certain individuals without ASD could likewise have a portion of these side effects. In any case, for those with ASD, these highlights can make life exceptionally extreme

Child - Human Age, Waving - Motion, Youngster, Blissful, Checking Camera out

Instances of social correspondence and social communication qualities associated with ASD incorporate

What is advanced mental imbalance?

Advanced mental imbalance is certainly not an acknowledged clinical finding. In any case, certain individuals utilise the expression to address a moderate sort of chemical imbalance that needs less measures of help. People on the gentle finish of the chemical imbalance range can talk, read, compose and deal with basic everyday errands. Suppliers used to term this Asperger disorder.

Chemical imbalance versus ADHD - is ADHD on the chemical imbalance range?

Chemical imbalance range infection and consideration shortfall/hyperactivity jumble (ADHD) have numerous similarities, despite the fact that ADHD isn't in the medically introverted range. The side effects of ADHD and mental imbalance once in a while cross-over. The two illnesses lead adolescents to have issues focusing, and both could harm their social capacities. These covering side effects can periodically prompt misleading conclusions.

ADHD and chemical imbalance are related hereditarily, also. Having one of these issues brings up your kid's probability of fostering the other. What's more, a kid with mental imbalance has a higher probability of having a direct relation with ADHD.

How normal is chemical imbalance?

As per the Places for Infectious prevention and Anticipation, ASD influences around 1 in each 44 8-year-old youngsters.

Mental imbalance in young men and kids doled out male upon entering the world (AMAB) is considerably more probable than chemical imbalance in young ladies and youngsters alloted female upon entering the world (AFAB) (AFAB). It's multiple times more normal in young men and kids AMAB than in young ladies and youngsters AFAB.

What are the side effects of mental imbalance?

Chemical imbalance side effects range from gentle to incredibly impairing, and each individual is unique. You ought to consider the accompanying indications of mental imbalance as potential markers that your kid might be in danger for the issue. Assuming that your child shows any of the accompanying early signs of chemical imbalance, reach out to their medical services proficient. They might suggest a reference for a chemical imbalance assessment.

Side effects of chemical imbalance remember difficulties for social connections, for example,

Your kid doesn't take a gander at you when you call out to them or answer conflictingly.

Your baby doesn't grin generally or show warm, cheerful articulations at 6 years old months.

Your baby doesn't participate in grinning, uttering sounds and making faces with you or others by the age of 9 months.

Your baby doesn't jibber jabber by the age of a year.

Your child doesn't utilise movements like coming to or waving at 12 years old months.

Your child plays no volatile games, similar to "surprise," by the age of a year.

Your baby says no words by the age of 16 months.

Your little child talks no significant, two-word phrases (excluding impersonation or rehashing) by the age of two years.

Any deficiency of discourse, chatter or interactive abilities.

Side effects of chemical imbalance likewise incorporate specific exercises, called confined or dull ways of behaving or interests:

Your adolescent consistently lines up toys or plays with toys the same way like clockwork.

Your adolescent should follow specific schedules or have solid responses to minuscule deviations in everyday practice.

Your youth has over the top or extremely remarkable interests.

Your kid's serious areas of strength have repugnances, for example, scorn of clear commotions, aversion of how specific garments fit or believe or profoundly particular eating.

Your youngster shows tactile looking for propensities, such as looking somewhere off to the side at things (looking) or sniffing or licking objects.

Social hardships, for example, disappointment and irate eruptions are very predominant in youngsters with mental imbalance range jumble (ASD) and can be challenging to control. It is essential to comprehend what is setting off the fury in a kid with ASD. On occasion it tends to be simply because the youngster can't make sense of his/her contemplations and sentiments to other people and feels disturbed. At different times it tends to be that the youngster with ASD loves 'equality,' in everyday practice and might be despondent due to changes in the day to day timetable or natural settings. Outrage may likewise be the result of an ailment when the youngster can't express torment, exhaustion, or actual inconvenience," says Dr Pratibha Singhi, Head, of the Branch of Paediatric Nervous system science, Amrita Medical clinic, Faridabad.

"Youngsters with mental imbalance for the most part have difficulties in friendly and relational abilities. Joined with a monotonous way of behaving and thinking, this prompts poor profound guidelines, fury, and impulsivity. It is vital to find the reason for forceful way of behaving, which can go from actual disease, distress, weakness, disturbance or ongoing change in conduct, tactile over-burden, to anything that prompts pressure and tension," says Dr Megha

Mahajan, Advisor - Youngster and Juvenile Psychiatry, Fortis Medical clinic, Bannerghatta Street.

"Kids with mental imbalance in India experience explicit trouble in dealing with their feelings, quiet rage. As per a new report, the predominance of mental imbalance in India is assessed to be 1 out of 68 kids, demonstrating an extraordinary requirement for successful resentment the board measures for this populace. In India, families and schools might defy deterrents in establishing a protected and steady climate for kids with mental imbalance. Low mindfulness and comprehension of mental imbalance might prompt an absence of facilities and devices for dealing with feelings appropriately. However, studies have demonstrated the way that giving a loosening up region to kids with chemical imbalance can extraordinarily diminish their feelings of anxiety and improve their close to home guideline," says Dr P. Venkat Swathi Ramani, Expert Paediatrician, CARE Medical clinics, Hello Sleuth City, Hyderabad.

TIPS FOR Medically introverted Children

"Quieting down a young person with mental imbalance can be undesirable and extreme. Look for clear triggers - In the event that one is remembered, one ought to try to eliminate it - for instance, on the off chance that it is an uproarious clamour, stop it. Check that the youngster isn't unwell or in distress. Assuming there is no clear reason and the youngster keeps on enduring fury explosions, different strategies should be endeavoured to decide the ones that turn out best for the kid. This is a process. It is critical to manage these to control unexpected eruptions of fury productively," says Dr Pratibha.

"Guardians ought to converse with the youngster utilising essential words and plain headings without judgement. Redirection and redirection are essential procedures to manage rage explosions. For more advanced youths, keep a rundown of interruptions open with the goal that those can be quickly used. A change in the air wherein the youth flies off the handle can be valuable," she says.

safe spot to vent outrage

"For a fairly more established youngster who will not tune in, one could likewise allow the kid securely to vent his/her sentiments in a protected region for instance shouting into a pad or involving it as a punching sack. Inevitably, the little child will feel depleted and start to quiet down. The kid could likewise be welcome to communicate his/her feelings by recording their sentiments. Never let the kid pull off shocking acts. In the event that fury is connected with basic melancholy, nervousness, or ADHD these ought to be satisfactorily treated," adds Dr Pratibha.

Preparing in Feeling Acknowledgment AND Interactive abilities

Preparing close to home identification and correspondence is one more key strategy for assisting youngsters with mental imbalance manage their fury.

"As per a review conducted in India, kids with mental imbalance who went through preparing in feeling acknowledgement and correspondence showed extensive additions in their capacity to direct their feelings. Visual devices, for example, temperament outlines and picture cards are especially valuable in assisting youngsters with chemical imbalance see and depict their sentiments. Interactive abilities preparing is particularly vital for kids with mental imbalance in India. Because of the particular social setting of India, social communications can be very hazardous for kids with mental imbalance. Studies have demonstrated that interactive abilities can extraordinarily further develop the social working and profound prosperity of youngsters with chemical imbalance in India," says Dr Ramani.

Organised Everyday practice
"Giving a trained timetable, profound marking, breaks, offering more secure choices for communicating dissatisfaction, and clear correspondence, can be valuable. Drugs ,likewise serve an essential job in managing outrage and viciousness

Dr Anju Sharma, Sound and Energy Master, TEDx Speaker, and Author of Brahm se Brahmand tak, says a lot of autistic youngsters are particularly sensitive to certain spectrums of sound and may get activated with some frequencies that act as painful sounds to them. She suggests sound treatment for them.

"Sound healing uses a range of distinct sounds that connect with the mind and body of a person. The frequency of particular sounds serves in holistic treatment to enhance emotional, physical and psychological wellness. Therefore people with autism are at risk of vulnerability which can reach to an extent of harm and mental disease over time. It is necessary to control and guide children to have a healthy and safe life," she explains.

Do I have autism?

Though most persons with autism receive their diagnosis during childhood, many don't until maturity. The most recent statistics suggest autism in adults affects more than 5 million persons in the U.S. or 2.21% of the population. Symptoms of autism in adulthood may include:

•Having difficulties comprehending what others are •experiencing or thinking.

•Excessive nervousness in social situations.

•Difficulty making friends or preferring to be on your own.

•Coming out as unpleasant, blunt or not interested in people yet not meaning to.

•Trouble expressing your feelings.

•Requirement for a constant routine and getting concerned if it changes.

•Avoiding eye contact.

•Issues with adequate spacing, such as coming too near to other people.

Autism in women and individuals AFAB can occasionally be different from autism in men and people AMAB.

Many women and people AFAB learn to mask the characteristics of autism to "fit into" society by emulating those who don't have autism. In addition, they're gentle and have to subside their emotions. Women and people AFAB appear to cope better in social circumstances than men and people AMAB. They also show less evidence of repeated activities.

If you suspect you may have autism, speak with a healthcare provider. Although there are adult autism tests available, only a certified specialist can identify the illness.

Can autism be prevented

You can't avoid autism, but you can lessen your risk of having a baby with the disorder by taking specific precautions, including:

1.Follow a healthy lifestyle: Make sure you see your healthcare provider regularly, consume a balanced diet and exercise. Obtain prenatal care, and take your provider's suggested vitamins and supplements.

2.Take care with medications: Ask your healthcare practitioner which medications are safe and which you should stop using throughout your pregnancy.

Don't drink: No sort and no amount of alcohol are safe during pregnancy.

3.Keep up with your vaccinations: Obtain all of your provider's recommended immunizations, including the German measles (rubella) vaccine, before you are pregnant. This vaccine can prevent rubella-associated autism.

What is the future for people with autism spectrum disorder (ASD)?

In many situations, the symptoms of ASD get milder as children get older. You may need to be flexible and ready to change treatment as needed for your child.

Individuals with ASD may go on to enjoy average lives, but there's typically a need for continuous care and support as they age. Their needs vary depending on the degree of their symptoms. For most, it's a lifetime condition that may require continuing support.

Chapter 3

Scientist Discovery of Autism

Autism Spectrum Research Neuroscience\sHuman Brain Neurons Connections

Researchers have uncovered a particular pattern of white matter connectivity in autistic individuals' brains that is different from that of those with developmental coordination problems. This points to a potential problem in earlier autism neuroscience research.

Recent research pinpoints three brain areas with hallmark connections in autistic individuals.

USC scientists uncover patterns of white matter connectivity limited to core autistic symptoms, pointing to a potential weakness in earlier autism neuroscience studies.

Scientists have uncovered a distinctive pattern of white matter connectivity exclusive to the brains of autistic persons distinct from that in the brains of people with developmental coordination disorder (DCD) (DCD).

These new study results were gathered from an international research team led by the University of Southern California (USC) (USC).

Developmental Coordination Disorder (DCD) is a neurodevelopmental disease classified in the DSM-V characterised by motor coordination deficits which severely impede daily living activities and involvement. The issues cannot be explained by another disorder and are already prevalent in early childhood. It is a persistent impairment that hampers coordination and is frequently nicknamed "clumsy child syndrome."

It is also known as developing motor coordination disorder, developmental dyspraxia or dyspraxia. About 2-6% of persons have DCD, with around four times as many males than females suffering from the illness.

Around 85% of autistic people have been or are likely to have been diagnosed with DCD, a condition that impairs learning and motor coordination. DCD can make it difficult to do simple tasks like typing, getting dressed, or walking, which may limit social interaction and enjoyment.

Because ASD and DCD are frequently co-occurring disorders, it is essential to distinguish between their brain activity patterns. This is because prior research on autism was thought to be only focusing on the disorder's core social-communication symptoms at the time it was undertaken.

According to Lisa Aziz-Zadeh, the study's senior author, "as the scientific community has learned more and more about DCD, we've discovered that white matter discrepancies previously observed in the autistic literature could potentially be linked to this underlying motor comorbidity." That's exactly what our team discovered, that many earlier research findings are likely not accurately reflecting the fundamental symptoms of autism but are instead more likely a reflection of co-occurring DCD.

Aziz-Zadeh holds dual appointments at the USC Dornsife College of Letters, Arts and Sciences' Brain and Creativity Institute and the Department of Psychology. She is an associate professor in the USC Chan Division of Occupational Science and

Occupational Therapy. She oversees research projects funded by the National Institutes of Health, the U.S. Department of Defense, and the Intelligence Advanced Research Projects Activity of the Office of the Director of National Intelligence at the USC Center for the Neuroscience of Embodied Cognition.

Diffusion-weighted MRI, a method for assessing functional brain connections, was used by Aziz-Zadeh and colleagues on children and teenagers aged 8 to 17 who were randomly assigned to one of three study groups: those with ASD, those with probable DCD, and typically developing people. The respondents' results from physical and social behaviour tests were also compared, assessed, and connected to the images. The researchers found that certain anatomical brain connection patterns that have historically been thought to be associated with autism are also present in DCD. The team was able to identify three white matter pathways, including the longitudinal fibres and u-fibres of the mid-cingulum, the corpus callosum forceps minor/anterior commissure, and the left middle cerebellar peduncle, that showed distinctly different connectivity, specific to the research participants with autism, as compared to the DCD and typically developing groups. The emotional performance and/or autism severity ratings of participants who were autistic also matched up with these changes.

According to Emily Kilroy, the first author of the article and a former post-doctoral researcher in Aziz-lab Zadeh's during the study's data collection period, "These results show that we can use advanced imaging to distinguish between autism's hallmark social symptoms and other motor-related symptoms at the level of brain anatomy." Although people are much more than just their brain structure, this level of anatomical clarity and specificity brings us one step closer to comprehending the molecular causes and symptoms of autism.

DIAGNOSTIC

Understanding the diagnosis and planning for the future in four steps

Up until maturity, Autism Spectrum Disorder (ASD) may go unnoticed or be incorrectly diagnosed. About getting a diagnosis as an adult, according to Ability Central.

a young brown man meets with a doctor

You might be looking for the following steps if you have read the Quick Facts, identified the signs of autism, and received a diagnosis.

Ability Central examines the first four actions to take as an older adolescent or adult after learning that you have Autism Spectrum Disorder (ASD), including:

•study as much as you can about autism.

•Recognizing the three levels of autism.

•get the help you require to proceed.

•Find out as much as you can about ASD.

The more you understand about autism, the easier it will be for you to realise that you are not alone. Funding for autism research has increased from 188 million to 290 million between 2016 and 2021. That suggests that we are learning new things every day. You are kept informed of the most recent findings in Portal research by Ability Central[GB6]. Additional fantastic sources are:

The manual used to make an ASD diagnosis is the DSM-5. This manual outlines the three stages of autism.

Level 1: Need for assistance

A person who meets the requirements for level 1 may struggle with social issues and need assistance. They might:

•I need help starting and maintaining conversations.

•must adhere to certain behavioural guidelines.

•Feel uneasy when their environment changes.

•I need assistance with planning and organisation.

Level 2: Requires substantial support

Those who meet the criteria for level 2 need further assistance. They might:

•a difficult conversation.

•I need assistance speaking clearly.

•Respond in a manner that neurotypical people would find surprising or inappropriate.

•have difficulty reading or using nonverbal cues, especially facial expressions.

Level 3: far more substantial help is needed

People who satisfy level 3 of the diagnostic criteria require the most support.

They might:

•Avoid others.

•Show limited to no interest in friends.

•Follow repetitious activities that seem weird to neurotypical folks.

Experiencing a high amount of distress if a situation demands them to adjust their attention or task.

Knowing how much support is needed based on the three diagnostic levels is critical to know how to progress.

Check for co-existing conditions.

A new study of legally independent autistic people indicated that participants diagnosed with autism at age 21 or later were 2.7 times more likely to experience co-occurring mood, anxiety, personality, or eating disorders than those identified with autism in childhood. Adulthood-diagnosed persons also reported greater lifetime psychiatric illnesses. Common co-existing conditions include:

Epilepsy

Sleep disorders

ADHD

Gastrointestinal diseases

Eating challenges

Obesity

Anxiety\sDepression

Bipolar disorder

It is crucial to keep under the supervision of a skilled physician who can assist diagnose and treat any coexisting diseases.

Create a support system for a prosperous future.

There are various benefits to pursuing an autism diagnosis as an adult. When an autistic adult acquires and communicates a diagnosis of ASD, it allows friends, family, and co-workers to arm themselves with knowledge of how to help them. In addition, it will assist the individual with the diagnosis to have a greater sense of self-identity that may boost their confidence.

Like with any new diagnosis, finding balance in the initial drive to investigate and learn about autism is vital. Rather than slipping into the trap of cognitive overload, it is vital to develop a support system. This includes:

Locate a person to chat with who can show compassion and help you set reasonable limits on your research time.

Scientists used stem cells from a patient with autism to build a lab-grown 'brain'

This enables them to examine if there are any variations in the brain of someone with the disease

The study revealed overactive neurons could contribute to the condition
Neurons were also not efficiently transferring signals to one another because circuits connecting neurons appeared to be broken
Brain-like organoids generated from cells of an individual with autism suggest overactive neurons in their brain may contribute to the illness.

Organoids are artificially generated masses of cells that resemble an organ and those used in a new study were designed to resemble the cerebral cortex, allowing scientists from the University of Utah Health to closely analyse this area of the brain that remains a mystery.
The seed-sized 'brains' were produced in a lab using stem cells from an individual with autism, allowing scientists to see how the neurons may change in someone with the illness.
Senior author Yueqi Wang said using the organoids could help researchers explore what happens at the early stages of neurological diseases before symptoms appear.

•The seed-sized mini-brains (shown) were produced in a lab using human stem cells from an individual with autism

•The seed-sized mini-brains (shown) were produced in a lab using human stem cells from an individual with autism

To make the organoids, the team looked at how the brain develops normally and urged the human stem cells to follow the same path.

The stem cells began as neuroepithelial cells, a unique stem cell type that produces self-organised structures, called neural rosettes, in a dish.

The cells were then permitted to grow on their own and over several months, the structures turned into spheres and developed in size and complexity at the same pace a brain would develop in a foetus.

Brain cells that offer humans better cognitive capacities over other animals are also linked to neurological illnesses including schizophrenia, autism and epilepsy, a new study suggests

Why you have all your best ideas in the SHOWER: Concentrating on a moderately-engaging task enhances your creativity more than just letting your mind roam freely, study reveals.

The team observed the organoid had overactive neurons that did not adequately connect with others. Shown is a slice of one of the organoids

The team observed the organoid had overactive neurons that did not adequately connect with others. Shown is a slice of one of the organoids

The formations featured an array of neuronal and other cell types present in the cerebral cortex, the outermost layer of the brain involved in language, emotion, thinking, and other high-level mental processes.

'We're beginning to comprehend how sophisticated neuronal structures in the human brain evolve from simple progenitors,' Wang added.

There is, however, controversy around lab-grown human 'mini-brains,' as some experts believe these organoids could eventually be placed in animals to better study neurological problems and create a 'Planet of the Apes' situation.

The warning comes from a team at Kyoto University who released a study in 2021 identifying several ethical problems that could develop with brain organoid research.

Tsutomu Sawai, an assistant professor at Kyoto University, said: 'This is still too futuristic, but it does not mean we should wait to settle on ethical norms.

Brain organoids, first developed in 2008, are 3D balls of brain-like tissue grown from stem cells — and frequently from that of humans.

Additional stem cell research includes using animal tissue to generate organoids, called 'xeno-organs, which are implanted into other animals.

The scientists spent five months cultivating the organoid. Shown is it maturing over one month

The scientists spent five months cultivating the organoid. Shown is it maturing over one month

For example, scientists successfully developed a mouse pancreas in a rat and vice versa.

This pioneering work is paving the path for the human pancreas to be produced in pigs that could subsequently be harvested for human organ transplantation.

The study emphasises, however, these animals would carry out their lives as organ farms for humans.

Nevertheless, Sawai noted there is a more important concern.

Sawai warns that doing so could result in the animals having improved powers, which may sound just like Planet of the Apes.

Planet of the Apes takes place on a faraway planet sometime in the future, where three astronauts become stranded and realise the world is ruled by intelligent apes.

The brain organoids have offered scientists a new means of studying the human brain - to better understand how it develops to learn how disorders occur.

"We don't know very much about the clinical profiles of these specific genetic variances that were disclosed as a part of this work, so it's going to be critical for us to understand more about individuals with those particular genetic changes," she said.

Behavioural examinations are needed to determine the clinical range of persons with these genetic abnormalities.

"As we learn more, this could help us address other issues regarding autism, including why some kids with autism are very high-functioning, while others need a lot more support," Kochel added.

Factor in the Underlying Causes of Autism Risk

Scientists at the Texas A&M University College of Medicine have made a groundbreaking discovery about the development of the brain. This new information contributes to our understanding of how the region of the brain that makes humans more intelligent than other mammals develops and offers insights into what causes intellectual problems, including autism spectrum disorders. For years, specialists have known that a thin layer of cells in the neocortex — the portion of the brain that regulates higher-order skills such as cognition, perception and language — is directly connected with intelligence in mammals. The bigger the surface area of the neocortex, the more highly developed the mental capacity of that organism. For example, the thickness of the human neocortex is only roughly three-fold bigger than that of mice. Nonetheless, the surface area of the human neocortex is 1,000-fold bigger than that of mice. Malformations in this area of the brain progress to developmental impairments that include autism spectrum disorders and intellectual disabilities.

What's not known is how the evolutionary expansion of this section of the brain proceeds preferentially in favour of expanding the surface area of the neocortex at the expense of increasing its thickness. How the initial populations of neural stem cells — the building blocks of the brain — spread themselves is a vital aspect of this process.

"There are many, what we'll call, separate processing units that are horizontally oriented in the neocortex. The more surface area you have, the more of these processing units you can accommodate," said Vytas A. Bankaitis, Distinguished Professor at the College of Medicine, E.L. Wehner-Welch Foundation Chair in Chemistry, and co-author of this study, which was published in Cell Reports. "The question is, why is the neocortical surface area so much higher relative to its thickness as one rises the mammalian evolutionary tree? Why do brain stem cells laterally distribute themselves as they grow and not pile on top of one other?"

This point is significant because when the cells do not spread out, but instead pile up, it generates a denser neocortex with a smaller surface area – a trait that has been identified in cases of intellectual impairment and even autism.

"One of the most researched genetic reasons for intellectual disability is a mutation in a gene that was formerly designated LIS1," said Zhigang Xie, assistant professor at the Faculty of Medicine and co-author of the study. "This genetic mutation will generate a smooth brain, which is connected with intellectual impairment. And one usual observation is that the neocortex of the patient is thicker than normal. There are also fairly new studies that indicate common characteristics in the brain of autism that include abnormally thickened regions of the neocortex in those individuals."

Scientists have known for some time that as neural stem cells divide, their nuclei migrate up and down within their anatomical space as a consequence of the cell cycle, a phenomenon called interkinetic nuclear migration. They do it by deploying a cytoskeletal network that acts like railway tracks with engines that move the nuclei up or down in a highly regulated manner. Although numerous concepts have been presented, it remains an enigma of why the nuclei move in this way, how this network of train tracks is managed, and what role interkinetic nuclear migration plays in the formation of the neocortex.

In their work, Xie and Bankaitis present solutions to these questions.

As for why, Bankaitis adds that when there are so many cells so close together in the embryonic stage of neocortical development, the movement of their nuclei up and down creates opposing upward and downward forces that spread the dividing neural stem cells out.

It would flatten and spread out. That's essentially how this works. You have an upward force and a downward force created by the movement of the nucleus that spreads these cells out."

Xie and Bankaitis also reveal how the cells do this by joining together many separate pathways that cooperate to "tell" the newborn neural stem cells where to go.

"I think for the first time, this truly pulls together molecules and signalling pathways that reveal how this process is managed and why it would be connected or associated with neurodevelopmental deficiencies," Bankaitis said. "We have taken a biochemical process, coupled it to a cell biology pathway, and related it to a signalling pathway that talks to the nucleus to stimulate the nuclear behaviour that generates a force that develops a sophisticated brain. It's now a complete circuit."

The outcome of this research disclosed an important element in the underlying causes of autism risk, intellectual disability and neural tube birth abnormalities. The new understanding of the basic principles determining the structure of the neocortex will also enable the design of in vitro brain culture systems that more precisely mimic the developmental processes of interest and increase the possibilities for neurological drug development.

"While there might show to be various reasons why a neocortex thickens instead of spreading, our work provides a new viewpoint on why patients with autism and intellectual difficulties generally display a thicker cortex,"

Scientists discover many new autism genes

These genes may provide vital clues to the causes of autism across the broad spectrum of the condition.

Numerous genes have previously been associated with autism; combined, they account for 20% of all cases. Most persons with these genes have severe forms of autism and other neurological problems like epilepsy and intellectual difficulties.

They discovered 60 genes associated with autism that may provide vital clues to the causes of autism across the full spectrum of the condition. Five genes have a more mild impact on autistic traits, including cognitive, than previously found genes.

"We need to undertake more extensive research with more individuals who possess these genes to understand how each gene contributes to the symptoms of autism, but we think these genes will help us untangle the scientific underpinnings that lead to most occurrences of autism."

"Many more moderate-effect genes remain to be uncovered, and finding them could help researchers better understand the biology of the brain and behaviour across the broad spectrum of autism."

Using Blood To Reveal the Mysteries of One Kind of Autism Autism Personality Test Unreliable

Autism spectrum disorder is a neurological and developmental illness. The disorder impacts how people connect, communicate, learn, and behave with others.

A study from the UC Davis MIND Center gives light on maternal autoantibody-related autism

A neurological disease termed autism spectrum disorder affects 1 in 44 kids in the United States. It has a vast spectrum of properties with varied intensities and origins. Maternal autoantibody-related autism spectrum disorder (MAR ASD) is one form of autism.

The presence of particular maternal immune proteins known as autoantibodies that respond to certain proteins found in the foetal brain distinguishes MAR ASD. Maternal autoantibodies (IgG) pass the placenta and enter the developing brain. Once there, they may affect the way the brain develops in youngsters, resulting in autism-like symptoms.

Two new UC Davis MIND Institute research are helping us learn more about this sort of autism. They observed evidence for predicted protein patterns in the blood of pregnant women, as well as associations between MAR ASD and increased intensities of autistic symptoms.

MAR ASD patterns successfully predict autism in previously diagnosed children. They studied maternal blood samples collected during pregnancy to see if they could validate the reported patterns. They sought to investigate if the patterns reliably predicted autism in youngsters. Their study findings were just published in the journal Molecular Psychiatry.

Previously, we discovered nine patterns associated with MAR ASD. In this study, we intended to investigate the accuracy of these patterns in predicting MAR ASD. To achieve that, we examined plasma from expectant moms, gathered by the Early Markers for Autism (EMA) study," said Van de Water, the study's principal author.

The study tested the plasma of 540 moms of autistic children, 184 mothers of kids with intellectual disability but no autism,

MAR ASD patterns linked to autism before birth

The MIND Institute's Judy Van de Water and a team of researchers found that autoantibody binding to nine unique combinations of proteins (known as MAR ASD patterns) successfully predicts autism in previously diagnosed children. They studied maternal blood samples collected during pregnancy to see if they could validate the reported patterns. They sought to investigate if the patterns reliably predicted autism in youngsters. Their study findings were just published in the journal Molecular Psychiatry.

Previously, we discovered nine patterns associated with MAR ASD. In this study, we intended to investigate the accuracy of these patterns in predicting MAR ASD. To achieve that, we examined plasma from expectant moms, gathered by the Early Markers for Autism (EMA)

study," said Van de Water, the study's principal author.

The study tested the plasma of 540 moms of autistic children, 184 mothers of kids with intellectual disability but no autism.

It found responsiveness to at least one of the nine MAR ASD patterns in 10% of the autistic population. This is compared with 4% of the intellectual disability group for particular patterns, and 1% of the general population group. Four patterns were found only in moms whose children were later diagnosed with autism, making those particular autoantibody patterns highly predictive.

The study also indicated that a mother with reactivity to any one of the nine MAR ASD patterns had roughly 8 times the likelihood of having an autistic kid.

Many MAR ASD types were strongly related to autism with intellectual disability. .

Earlier research revealed the MAR subtype of autism in 20% of a Northern California sample of autistic kids Nevertheless, until recently, this sort of autism has not been investigated in any state outside California.

A team of researchers led by Kathleen Angkustsiri studied MAR ASD in two new clinical sites: the Children's Hospital of Philadelphia (CHOP) and Arkansas Children's Hospital and Research Institute (ACHRI) (ACHRI). Their study, published in The Journal of Developmental and Behavioral Pediatrics, recruited 68 moms of autistic children ages 2-12 years. The mothers supplied blood samples and completed behavioural questionnaires about their children.

Autism Child Assistance

Early diagnosis provides for individualised child support. Credit: University of California – Davis Health

68 mothers of autistic children between the ages of 2 and 12 were included in their study, which was published in The Journal of Developmental and Behavioral Pediatrics. The mothers gave blood samples and answered questions concerning their kids' behaviour.

Autism Child Support

An early diagnosis enables tailored child support. Credit: Davis Health at the University of California

Also, information from the kids' clinical diagnostic exams was included in the study.

In all, 23.5% of the blood samples were determined to be MAR positive (+MAR), indicating the presence of autoantibodies that react with recognized MAR ASD protein sequences.

According to Angkustsiri, "our study revealed comparable MAR ASD frequencies in two other states identical to what we identified in Northern California." The principal author of the study is Angkustsiri, an associate professor of developmental-behavioural

paediatrics at the UC Davis Children's Hospital and the UC Davis MIND Institute. This implies that the prevalence of MAR ASD is constant across various demographic groups and geographical contexts.

MAR ASD and autistic symptoms

The study also looked at the relationship between the severity of autism and MAR ASD. Research demonstrated that kids with +MAR antibodies had higher autism severity scores than kids with -MAR antibodies. It found no appreciable variations in their Intellect, ability to adapt, or odd behaviour.

According to Angkustsiri, "MAR ASD positive may be associated with more severe autism behaviours." "These findings were validated by both the SCQ submitted by parents and the ADOS evaluated by doctors. "

It is necessary to conduct more research to determine why mothers produce these antibodies and how long they may last. To determine whether a kid has autism before symptoms appear, testing for MAR ASD patterns can be used. To give physicians more tools for an earlier diagnosis of ASD, researchers hope to create a reliable clinical test.

Based on the child's skills and unique challenges as well as the type of autism, Van de Water remarked, "We hope our study can help build more customised services."

Chapter 4

Dispelling the autism myth

Vaccination does not cause autism. A brief study in 1998 revealed a relationship between vaccines and autistic spectrum conditions. The paper was evaluated further and retracted. In addition, the author's medical licence was revoked owing to fabricated information.

Since then, numerous studies have debunked a connection between autism and the measles, mumps and rubella (MMR) vaccine.

Almost 2,000 of the kids were labelled as being at risk for autism because they had a sibling who had already received a diagnosis. The MMR vaccine did not raise the risk of autism spectrum condition, according to the study.

Information on vaccines

Viruses or bacteria that are dead or weakened are used in vaccinations to assist your body mount an immune response. Compared to acquiring immunity through natural infection, these vaccinations greatly lower the risk of disease and consequences while assisting children in developing natural immunity.

The majority of the time, side effects are modest and include discomfort at the injection site, lumps or bumps there, weariness, agitation, headaches, decreased appetite, or low-grade fever.

safeguarding your child and others

The advantages of becoming immunised outweigh any potential risks for almost all youngsters. Children frequently experience considerably more severe effects from vaccine-preventable diseases, which can occasionally result in life-long problems, hospitalizations, and even death.

Not vaccinating your children also increases the risk to people around them. Some children cannot be vaccinated owing to medical reasons. Their sole protection is herd immunity, where everyone surrounding an at-risk person is vaccinated against infection. This minimises the risk to the exposed person.

While evaluating your child's health and safety, remember to factor in the importance and requirement of adequate childhood vaccines. Not only are you safeguarding your child, but also you will be defending your community.

It is a truth that acting in one's perceived self-interest is not necessarily in one's self-interest. Probably nowhere is this truer in contemporary public health than for the topic of the measles-mumps-rubella (MMR) inoculation and persisting suspicions about a probable connection with autism. Although each of these 3 diseases had been controlled in the United States with the widespread use of the MMR vaccine, in the past decade those gains have been receding. Even though the United States has had fewer than 50 measles cases each year throughout the preceding decade (mainly imported from other nations), 156 cases have already been identified in the first 6 months of 2011. European countries such as England, Wales, Italy, France, Spain, and Germany are also experiencing major increases in measles epidemics.

Why should we be concerned? Measles is the most transmissible human illness known. Even with current medical care, around 1 of every 3000 infected persons die, and many more are hospitalised or otherwise damaged as a result. Population coverage (herd immunity) needs to be more than 96% to prevent epidemics. In addition, measles is a disease for which eradication is both achievable and intended, a goal that simply cannot be realised given present vaccine coverage levels.

This expected cycle of lowering coverage levels, followed by outbreaks of disease, has occurred because of decreased public faith in the safety of the MMR vaccine. In large part, this has resulted from false allegations that the vaccine plays a role in the development of autism, a theory espoused by Andrew Wakefield. No solid scientific evidence, however, supports the notion that the MMR vaccine causes autism, and indeed, national medical authorities and scientific professional organisations have universally repudiated that assertion. More than 20 studies have revealed no indication of the relationship between the receipt of the MMR vaccine and autism symptoms. In fact, Britain's General Medical Council decided after its hearings that Wakefield was guilty of dishonesty and serious professional misconduct concerning his MMR-autism research. 8 More recently, the editor of the British Medical Journal wrote a commentary declaring that Wakefield's MMR autism research was false.

Why in the face of nearly 2 dozen studies and every scientific body denying such an MMR-autism connection does this myth persist? I and others have written extensively about the anti vaccine movement and its deleterious effect on vaccine decision-making and on the role of the media in creating fear. A recent case is worth analysing. The Pace Environmental Law Review released an article claiming that a "preliminary evaluation" of cases reimbursed through the Vaccine Injury Compensation Program (VICP) "suggests that vaccine-induced encephalopathy and a seizure disorder may be related to autism." Even though several studies have failed to uncover such a correlation, enormous media attention was given to this piece, certainly producing further anxiety and confusion in the minds of the people. To the degree, the authors intended to argue that vaccines like MMR cause or contribute to autism, their conclusion is not only wrong but also at variance with the work of the VICP itself.

Such a judgement cannot be reconciled with the overwhelming corpus of scientific knowledge. The Centers for Disease Control and Prevention (CDC), for example, has concluded that "carefully executed scientific studies have established no association between MMR vaccine and autism" and "no higher risk of [autism spectrum disorder] related with receipt of thimerosal-containing vaccines."(Notice, thimerosal includes ethylmercury, another target of those who attack the safety of the MMR vaccine.) Similarly, the Institute of Medicine stated that the "body of epidemiological evidence justifies denial of a causal connection between the MMR vaccine and autism," and "between thimerosal-containing vaccinations and autism." Several organisations, like the American Academy of Pediatrics, have reached similar conclusions.

More significantly for current purposes, the VICP itself—after conducting the most extensive and elaborate fact-finding proceedings in its history—concluded there is no causal connection between childhood vaccinations and autism. After evaluating the data, one special master noted that "numerous medical studies … done by medical specialists worldwide have come down strongly against" the argument "that the MMR vaccine can cause autism." In another case, the special master determined that "the evidence is overwhelmingly opposed to the petitioners' contentions … that thimerosal-containing vaccines can contribute to the cause of autism." The authors of the Pace Environmental Law Review article claim that there may be a connection between vaccines and autism despite these epidemiological studies and the specific findings of the VICP by referring to isolated language found in a few of the VICP's decisions over the course of the past two decades and parent interviews in some settled cases (suggesting a conspiratorial plot). Yet, their attempts to draw conclusions from their subpar analysis misunderstand how the functions.

The no-fault compensation VICP was adopted by Congress to enable damage payments to be made "quickly, easily, and with certainty and generosity."

The Vaccine Injury Table, which covers all immunizations authorised by the Advisory Committee on Immunization Practices for routine administration to children, forms the foundation of how the VICP operates in part. The exact conditions that may be related to the vaccinations listed in the table have been identified by the secretary of the Department of Health and Human Services. The program offers two ways to compensate a claimant who requests compensation

: (1) by demonstrating that she/he received a "table vaccine" and that it caused the subsequent injury or death, which must be proven by a preponderance of the evidence, or

(2) by demonstrating that she/he received a "table vaccine" and that it caused one of the conditions listed on the table, known as a "table injury," within a certain time frame.

It's important to note that a claimant can collect compensation under the VICP without having to prove that the vaccination caused the alleged injury; instead, the claimant only needs to show that one of the listed conditions occurred during the authorised time after the immunisation.

Autism is not now listed as a specified injury and never has been. However, the writers of the Pace Law Review article cannot find any instances in which the VICP has determined that a vaccine caused autism, even for injuries that are not on the table. The Health administration "has maintained and continues to maintain the view that vaccines do not cause autism, and has never ruled in any case that autism was caused by immunisation."

Hence, despite the public attention given to the Pace Law Review study, its conclusions are false, and requests for deeper investigation into a possible link between the MMR vaccine and autism are incorrect. It is crucial to concentrate resources on providing meaningful support for those with autism at a time when competition for scarce federal research funding is fierce. This can be done by figuring out what causes autism and how to lessen its symptoms so that anyone who has the condition can live a healthier and more fulfilling life. Thus, it is past time to put to rest the myth that vaccines are to blame.

How, then, should the general public, the press, medical experts, decision-makers, and other interested parties react? The way forward is clear. The theory linking the MMR vaccine to autistic issues is devoid of solid evidence and must be dismissed as there has been no credible evidence to support it during the past 13 years. The public health issue of autism must be addressed by increasing research funding and allocating that money to the examination of workable causal hypotheses. It is risky and irresponsible to keep investing money in fruitless efforts to demonstrate a link to the MMR vaccine when numerous high-quality scientific studies conducted over many years and in several different countries have failed to detect even the slightest connection and in the face of biologic non plausibility.

The small group of people who assert such connections, who lack new or reliable data, and whose assumptions and hypotheses have been disproven, must at some point, a point I believe we have well passed, simply be ignored by scientists, the general public, and, most importantly, the media, no matter how fervent their beliefs to the contrary. Such people are, at best, denialists and, at worst, dangerous. 27, 28, 29 Unfortunately, celebrities who speak out about an autism-MMR link have received far more attention from the media than they should have, and the general public has mistakenly assumed that celebrities have more authority because they are famous. Those who want to talk about the subject further have not overlooked such an occurrence. In response to the discovery that both Andrew Wakefield and his claim that a connection between autism and the MMR vaccine had been disproven, J. Hanlon, co-founder of Generation Rescue (an organisation that advocates for an autism-MMR vaccine link), stated that to those who believe vaccines cause autism,

Demanding responsible and scientifically sound media reporting is a crucial next step. It is just irresponsible and cruel to not only the general public but especially to people and families who have a loved one with autism to continue widely disseminating dramatic "revelations" concerning the MMR vaccine and autistic disorders, conspiracy theories, and other false information. By itself, continuing such scientifically incorrect information needlessly encourages concerns and mistrust about the safety of vaccinations, and leads to parental confusion and decisions to choose not to immunise their children—with predictable and awful results.

The deep separation between those who agree with the scientific practices and evidence and those who do not and merely choose to reject the facts cannot, however, be remedied by any magical solutions.

Reason and education can only go so far in combating risk perception and cognitive biases; at some point, usually when the costs to society are obvious (such as protecting the most vulnerable from highly contagious diseases), more action must be done and laws passed. For instance, we adopt laws regulating the wearing of seat belts in order to protect drivers, their passengers, and the general public. We must have a conversation about equivalent vaccination limits that are restricted to the specific and defined goal of preventing the spread of infectious diseases that are dangerous to the public's health.

There is no known scientific link between receiving the MMR vaccine and the later emergence of autism, according to everyone who has followed the scientific process of discovery, research, and proof. The trial has ended and the jury has returned. As evidenced by the current measles outbreaks in the United States and Europe, choosing not to immunise children with the MMR vaccination because of fear of such an association—rather than compelling scientific evidence—places children and others at significant danger. It is simply untrue for vaccination nihilists to continue making these claims, because they promote agendas other than the general welfare. The conspiracy theorists and anti-vaccine groups should now be dismissed, just as sane people condemn those who continue to believe that the earth is flat or that the US moon landing in 1969 did not take place.

However, millions of children's health in the United States and around the world are being put at unnecessary and real risk through continued deliberate misinformation and discredited unscientific beliefs, and that should be illegal. There is no law against being foolish, and there is no vaccine against ignorance.

—

Chapter 6

Asperger's syndrome

It is a condition that affects a person's capacity for effective communication and social interaction.

On the autism spectrum, Asperger's syndrome is a disorder with typically greater functioning.

Those with Asperger's syndrome, formerly known as autism spectrum disorder, may benefit from early diagnosis and use of support networks. Individualised education programs (IEPs) may be available for school-aged children who have this condition (IEPs).

Testing and Diagnose Administration and Therapy Living amidst

The broad diagnosis known as autism spectrum disorder (ASD) includes Asperger's syndrome, often known as high-functioning autism (ASD). Since 2013, the Diagnostic and Statistical Manual of Mental Disorders, Fifth Edition (DSM-5) revised criteria have replaced Asperger's syndrome with the more inclusive diagnosis of ASD. Testing and Diagnose Administration and Therapy Living amidst

How a Diagnosis is Made

See a paediatrician if you spot any symptoms in your child. They can suggest one of the following mental health professionals who focuses in ASDs:

Psychologist:. They identify and address emotional and behavioural issues.

child neurology specialist: They deal with brain disorders.

child development specialist. They are experts in developmental concerns, including speech and language disorders.

Psychiatrist: They are knowledgeable about mental health issues and are able to recommend medications to treat them.

A collaborative approach is frequently used to address the illness. This implies that you might take your child to more than one doctor for treatment.

The doctor will inquire about your child's behaviour and ask questions like:

How does your child communicate?

 When did they start speaking?

Do they have any specific interests or activities in mind?

Do they communicate with people well, and do they have friends?

.

Can Asperger's syndrome be treated with medication?

Some individuals with Asperger's syndrome or associated disorders can lead fulfilling lives without taking any drugs. The symptoms you or your kid are experiencing will determine whether or not your doctor will recommend medication. Reducing the amount of medications you or your child use can also be accomplished by concentrating on addressing only the symptoms that are a concern.

Strong Asperger's symptoms or conditions connected to it can be controlled with certain types of medicines. These medicines consist of:

Antidepressants (SSRIs or selective serotonin reuptake inhibitors) (SSRIs or selective serotonin reuptake inhibitors).

Anti-psychotics.

medication for attention deficit disorder.

Discuss if these and other medications are appropriate for you or your kid with your doctor because they may have serious side effects.

Treatment

As every child is unique, there isn't a single strategy that works for all of them. To discover the right treatment, your doctor may need to try a few different approaches.

Treatments may consist of:

socialisation instruction: Therapists work with your child one-on-one or in groups to help them learn how to interact with others and express themselves in more suitable ways. The most effective way to learn social skills is to imitate common behaviour.

Language and speech treatment: Your child's communication skills will benefit from this. For instance, kids will learn to speak with a natural up-and-down pattern rather than a flat tone. Also, they will learn how to maintain a two-way conversation and recognize social indicators like eye contact and hand gestures.

Behavioural and cognitive therapy (CBT): It aids in your child's mental transformation so they can better manage their emotions and habitual behaviours. Outbursts, meltdowns, and obsessions will be easier for them to control.

training and instruction for parents: Many of the methods your child is taught will be given to you so you may work on social skills with your child at home. In order to cope with the difficulties of having a member of the family with Asperger's, some families also consult a counsellor.

Applied behaviour analysis: It's an approach that develops positive social and communication skills in your child — and discourages conduct you'd rather not see. The therapist will utilise praise or other "positive reinforcement" to get results.

Medicine.

There aren't any medications approved by the FDA that particularly treat Asperger's or autism spectrum illnesses. Certain drugs, nevertheless, can help with linked symptoms including despair and anxiety. Your doctor may prescribe some of these:

Selective serotonin reuptake inhibitors (SSRIs) (SSRIs)

Antipsychotic medications

Stimulant medications
With the correct treatment, your kid can learn to handle some of the social and communicative issues they confront. They can do well in school and go on to thrive in life.

How can children with Asperger's syndrome be more comfortable at school?

Children and teens with Asperger's syndrome and similar illnesses often suffer at school. It can be tough to learn while having problems focusing or staying calm. To help them learn more readily, certain children with these disabilities can benefit from (or need) special education or accommodations at school.

For example, parents and teachers can work together to design an individual education program (IEP) (IEP). Based on your child's symptoms, their school will decide if an IEP is needed. IEPs enable a more suited teaching environment including:

•Routine daily routines (to help students focus and keep calm) (to help students focus and keep calm).

•'Milestone' academic goals (passing physical education, or earning a specific score on important tests) (passing physical education, or getting a certain score on major tests).

•Study aids or tailored lesson plans (using headphones with audio courses, for example) (using headphones with audio lessons, for example).

•Social skills (joining gatherings and not interrupting others) (joining groups and not interrupting others).

Self-control strategies (not having tantrums or striking) (not having tantrums or hitting).

Depending on their difficulties at school, children may also be eligible for special education programs like counselling and special nutritional needs. Learn about IEPs and other at-school support by contacting your child's teacher, guidance counsellor or principal.

Is there a cure for Asperger's syndrome?

Today there is no cure for ASD. Nor are there any home remedies or herbal supplements shown to cure Asperger's syndrome or associated diseases.

However various non-surgical treatments exist to help manage several of the condition's symptoms including depression, social anxiety and obsessive-compulsive disorder (OCD) (OCD).

Therapy (including speech therapy for young children and cognitive behavioural therapy for adults) is another useful solution for investigating ways to improve the quality of life for you, your kid or your students.

Several persons with Asperger's syndrome believe that counselling helps them to manage their symptoms or other concerns. Treatment providers for children and adults with Asperger's syndrome include:

Physical therapists: Physical therapy can assist improve coordination and balance. It can also aid kids to focus better when presented with distracting noises or visuals.

Speech therapists: Speech therapy can enhance your ability to talk effectively and at suitable volumes.

Occupational therapists: Occupational therapy can help you gain job skills needed to become and stay independent.

Family or relationship therapists: This sort of therapy can help children and adults establish stronger relationships with friends and loved ones.

Your healthcare physician might provide you with advice or referrals to these kinds of therapy.

living with autism

How can someone with Asperger's syndrome live the greatest life possible?

Many people diagnosed with Asperger's syndrome and similar conditions attain success in their life. Others may need some aid in finding or keeping work, living arrangements and social ties. If you have Asperger's syndrome, you might function best with controlled, predictable environments and routines.

Many adolescents, teens and adults with Asperger's syndrome benefit from social skills groups and behaviour interventions, like those given by Applied Behavioral Analysis (ABA) (ABA). This sort of behavioural treatment tries to teach beneficial behaviours in everyday life

Chapter 7

Creating a Neurodiverse Environment

These are six methods that foster neurodiversity at work and home Neurodiversity refers to the limitless heterogeneity in human neurocognitive functioning Image: Unsplash / deep mind We are each surrounded by people that think and absorb information differently than ourselves. Such is the case for my 21-year-old daughter and me. Early in her youth, she began encountering issues with reading and spelling. The reasons for her challenges became evident when we subsequently realised she had dyslexia. As a parent, I soon understood that although I saw words that comprised the English language, she saw curves and lines that were more like artistic shapes.

Even now, as she thrives in the face of dyslexia, we form a terrific team. I may be able to spell words faster, but she surpasses me with her extraordinary artistic, inventive, and creative skills.

Parents at home, and even managers at work, may have comparable relationships with someone who is neurodivergent. 15 to 20% of the world's population is neurodiverse, including up to 10% of people who have dyslexia, 5% of people who are diagnosed with ADHD, and 2% diagnosed with autism.

As a parent and company leader, I've learned how to encourage teamwork in a neurodiverse workplace. I've also leveraged the values and principles of Agile and the practices of Scrum to foster alignment and avoid confusion for team members who are neurodiverse. Companies that accept neurodiverse personnel and support agility can build an inclusive and collaborative workplace for all their team members.

Understanding and valuing neurodiversity at home and work

Neurodiversity refers to the limitless heterogeneity in human neurocognitive functioning. There is no standard for a healthy or normal brain and how it should take in information and produce meaning.

Like many humans, our kids struggle with executive functioning skills. They have to work very hard or may even be unable to plan, keep organised, commence projects, maintain attention, and manage time.

Giving children frameworks or structures at home,
•lists and timers
•Cycles, logs, and check-ins every day
•posting schedules and calendars in graphic form
•many calls, mails, and prods in person
•Teams of programmers, engineers, designers, analysts, and technicians of all stripes have surrounded me at work. These coworkers frequently have extraordinary cognitive abilities and professional capabilities since they examine and process information significantly differently from one another. Many have openly discussed their experiences with ASD or ADHD.

Several neurodiverse people work in the fields of science, technology, engineering, and maths. According to data, people who are autistic study in all professions, but they enrol in STEM at far higher rates than the overall population—34% of autistic college students enrol in the field, compared to 22% of the general population.

The teams that have created many of the greatest inventions of the last 20 years have relied heavily on agile attitudes, concepts, and practices. This approach contains lessons that are much more significant than your most recent go-to-market plan.

Techniques for Neurodivergent Teams

We've discovered and embraced behaviours, patterns, and practices as I've worked with neurodivergent engineers that make life better for everyone on the team, whether at home or at work. Examples of this include:

Establish patterns: Make sure the collaborative team activities within each iteration follow the same pattern and take place on the same days by planning and carrying out the work in iterations of a constant length, such as two weeks.

What is success? Describe each task in a way that fits the needs of the team, placing special attention on describing how the team will determine when a task is acceptable and what to do about it.

Bring about transparency: Make the list of tasks in the backlog public, give the team control over how to finish the work, and hold them responsible for deciding how much of the list they will complete inside the iteration.

every day: A brief daily standing meeting encourages communication and enables the team to evaluate success and adjust strategies as necessary.

Examine and adjust: Incorporate continuous improvement by reflecting collectively as a team on the successes and challenges of the previous iteration and developing an experiment that could enhance things in the upcoming one.

Create bonds: Be proactive about forming bonds and growing as a team; encourage the emergence and maintenance of reliable alliances; and avoid frequently changing the team's composition.

Scrum before you go to sleep?

When my kids were younger, putting them to bed involved a hectic dance between parents and kids that frequently resulted in irritation. But once we used a condensed version of the aforementioned cases, things significantly got better. It was known as "Bedtime Scrum," and it was based on a chart that we created and posted in the hallway next to the children's beds. Two columns, one with a red light and the other with a green light, were displayed on the chart. Finally, we added cards to the red light column that featured images of each evening chore. The card for a bedtime story was the last one on the list of cards.

Within two nights, the children realised that they needed to finish all the tasks on the cards and move them to the column with the green light in order to receive a bedtime story. They took great pleasure in completing each task on the chart quickly. The outcomes were fantastic! My role quickly changed from a frantic bedtime goalie to a peaceful observer waiting for story time as the small ones took care of their own obligations. For this application at work, the same is true.

maximising diversity over time
Even if someone holds opinions that differ from your own, that doesn't mean their ideas aren't worthwhile. It doesn't imply that someone's contribution to solving an issue is less valuable just because they approach it differently than you do. As leaders in the commercial world, we must employ inquiry, see past the barriers brought about by our prejudices and cultural preconceptions, and recognize the potential in a neurodivergent individual.

The good news for today's managers, supervisors, and C-suite executives is that many business leaders are attracted to the Agile frameworks and their advantages. These leaders can create a diverse environment that is safe, collaborative, and effective if they lean into these values with an inclusive mentality.

How to create a work environment that values neurodiversity

A corporation can greatly benefit from having people that can contribute to thinking beyond the box.

In the past year, AJ received diagnoses for Asperger's syndrome and dyslexia. He believes that his atypical brain structure helps him in his job as a principal software engineer at the UK's Defence Science and Technology Laboratory.

"The more diverse opinions, ideas, and ways of approaching things you can bring together, the better. We're trying to understand things and solve issues.

International Autism Awareness Day is observed on April 2; this year's theme is Inclusive Quality Education for All. Children with autism have been disproportionately affected by the COVID-19 pandemic's interruption of education and support systems.

According to the UN, people with autism spectrum disorders can "fulfil their potential and achieve sustainable success in the labour market" with access to education, vocational training, and lifelong learning opportunities.

However, as evidenced by employment statistics, neurodiverse individuals—those with unique thought processes and diagnoses including autism, dyspraxia, dyslexia, and ADHD—frequently face bias, with businesses emphasising the drawbacks of neurodiversity at work rather than its advantages.

"It's not about getting rid of it or treating it," says AJ. Giving them the resources they require to reach their full potential is important.

Why having a diverse workforce is important

Deloitte, a consulting and auditing organisation, estimates that 10% to 20% of people worldwide are neurodivergent.

According to the World Health Organization's most recent statistics, one in 100 children worldwide have autism, but for many people, like AJ, the condition is not discovered until much later in life. According to the US Centers for Disease Control and Prevention, autism spectrum disorder, or ASD, affects one in every 44 children in the US.

According to Deloitte, the majority of those with autism (85%) are unemployed, compared to 4.2% of the general population, despite autism's high prevalence in the US.

AJ continues, "I think there are many assumptions about all kinds of neurodiversity. Many often assume that people with dyslexia can't read, and that those with autism and Asperger's syndrome lack any social skills and can't function in the real world.

None of those, in my opinion, are true. If you've met one neurodiverse person, you've met one neurodiverse person, according to an adage. We are all unique in the same way that everyone else is.

Several businesses, including Deloitte, Microsoft, SAP, JPMorgan Chase, and EY, have established neurodiversity hiring initiatives in response to their recognition of the skills that neurodiverse individuals may offer to the workplace.

 a group of companies collaborating to "provide awareness, knowledge, and supportive structures that give neurodivergent individuals the opportunity to develop and realise their full potential."

According to the Harvard Business Review, applicants for SAP's Autism at Work project in 2013 included those with dual degrees and master's degrees in electrical engineering and economic statistics, yet many of them had previously been denied employment in occupations that required their skills.

Among many other qualities, neurodiverse employees hired through these programs are praised for their attention to detail, pattern recognition, inferential reasoning, mathematics and coding skills, timeliness, and for providing original, creative solutions.

What businesses can do to encourage neurodiversity

Deloitte contends that leaders need to be more open about their personal lives. According to Jones Chambers, the former CEO of technology giant Cisco, one in four CEOs has dyslexia. Chambers is one of the more approachable neurodiverse executives, along with Virgin Group founder Richard Branson.

Deloitte argues that if leaders self-identify as neurodivergent, the rest of the workforce will feel free to do the same.

companies need to establish a culture where both neurodivergent and neurotypical employees can succeed. Avoiding a one-size-fits-all approach when dealing with staff is part of this.

Instead, managers should "discover each professional's best working and learning styles and adjust their style accordingly."

One professor of neurodivergent students who stressed to Deloitte the need to be more specific with directions, including adding verbs like "read chapter 1" and "solve problems 1 to 8," said that small changes to communication can go a long way.

Offering mentors and friends, as well as increasing flexibility, especially with regard to hybrid working, are important ways to promote an inclusive culture that can boost output and loyalty.

Common worries for neurodivergent workers may interfere with conventional HR procedures, but they can inevitably make the workplace a better, safer, and more welcoming place for everyone, as Deloitte concludes.

Meet Jones . He's a master at data analytics. His combination of intellectual competence and software development skills is exceedingly unique. His Résumé shows two master's degrees, both with honours. An obvious guy for a tech corporation to scoop up, right?

Until lately, no. Before Jones ran upon a corporation that had begun experimenting with new approaches to talent, he was unemployed for more than two years. Other companies he had dealt with sorely required the skills he possessed. But he was unable to pass the hiring process.

After observing Jones for a while, you would begin to understand why. He does seem... strange. He always has headphones on, and he rarely looks directly at people when they speak to him. Every ten minutes or so, he leans down to tie his shoelaces because he finds it difficult to focus when they are loose. Jones , however, is the person in the division who is most productive when things are tight. He works hard and doesn't like to take pauses. He doesn't like them, but his appointed office "buddy" has finally convinced him to do them. Jones " is a composite of folks with autism spectrum disorders, whose privacy we wanted to safeguard. He serves as a model for participants in the initiatives of trailblazing businesses that have started looking for "neurodiverse" talent.

Many people resemble Jones . According to the Centers for Disease Control and Prevention, there are currently 1 in 42 boys and 1 in 189 girls in the United States who have autism. Corporate programs could also be expanded to include persons with dyspraxia (a physical ailment with a neurological basis), dyslexia, ADHD, social anxiety disorders, and other diseases, even if they have so far only targeted autistic people. Research shows that some illnesses, like autism and dyslexia, can grant great aptitude in pattern recognition, memory, or mathematics. Many people with these diseases have higher-than-average abilities. Yet, persons who are afflicted occasionally have trouble fitting the criteria set forth by potential employers.

To activate or use their abilities to the fullest, neurodiverse people frequently require professional accommodations, such as headphones to minimise auditory overstimulation. They occasionally display bothersome quirks. The potential rewards are significant and the adjustments and challenges are frequently controllable. But in order to reap the benefits, most businesses would need to alter their hiring, vetting, and career development procedures to take into account a wider notion of talent.

Many more are starting up or conducting exploratory research, including Caterpillar, Dell Technologies, Deloitte, IBM, JPMorgan Chase, and UBS. We have spoken with representatives from Microsoft, Willis Towers Watson, and EY, and have had extensive access to the neurodiversity programs at SAP, HPE, and Specialisterne (the Danish consulting firm that developed such programs).

Benefits of Establishing a Neuro Inclusive Workplace

DE&I has moved to the forefront of the corporate agenda as businesses realise that diverse and inclusive environments are typically also the most productive, successful, and in-demand workplaces. Nonetheless, despite the general push for better opportunity equality for all underrepresented groups, those with neurological disabilities can still be left behind.

To encourage workforce diversity and "better integrate and leverage the full potential of neurodivergent workers," the consultant suggests concentrating on three key areas.

It begins by taking a closer look at the hiring procedures, which might be filled with unintentional biases and algorithms that are developed using "neurotypical" candidate data.

It is possible to alter interview procedures to make candidates feel less anxious. For instance, Microsoft arranges hiring occasions that last for several days so that applicants can showcase their skills..

The word "neurodiverse" refers to those with attention, communication, visual, or physical problems that go beyond neurotypical cognition, and it is suggested that up to 5% of the world's population fits this description. Autism (ASD), ADHD, dyslexia/dyscalculia, and Tourette's syndrome are all common disorders.

Despite the fact that neurodivergent individuals' abilities might naturally range widely, even those with great talent may not meet the hiring requirements of potential employers. For instance, 78% of adults with autism are unemployed, which is the highest rate of any one category, according to UK statistics.

Untapped capacity

These data imply that companies are ignoring the novel viewpoints that individuals from neuro-minority groups might offer to the workplace.

The CEO of Seccl Technologies, Sam Handfield-Jones, has ADHD.
"Diversity of all kinds needs to be promoted at work. You continue acting in the same way if everyone has the same appearance, experiences, or viewpoints. Neurodiversity provides organisations with essential abilities to stay competitive, innovate, and adapt in a rapidly changing world. Nevertheless, because some of the behaviours that neurodiverse people are known for don't cleanly fit into conventional views of what constitutes a good employee - such as outstanding communication skills, teamwork, and emotional intelligence - they are frequently screened out of consideration.
After receiving a neurodiversity (ADHD) diagnosis the previous year,

KK Harris, Executive Coach Director at Talking Talent, now assists organisations in hastening the progress of under-represented talent. Making the world more accessible for people who are neurodiverse and respecting their learning disabilities and worldview will be beneficial in every profession, according to research. Yet, by focusing too much on the stigma associated with neurodiversity, employers overestimate the level of help that talent with neurodiverse backgrounds requires and inevitably overlook excellent candidates.

fostering a diverse workplace culture

While neurodiversity benefits businesses by spurring innovation, it also enhances workplace cultures by serving as an example of the distinctive skills and behaviours that contribute to a sense of belonging and purpose, which in turn has an effect on the larger workforce.

Audeliss and INvolve are two companies with a DE&I focus that were founded by Suki Sandhu, OBE. Suki is certain that neurodiverse talent can represent the new viewpoints that aid businesses in becoming much more aware of their larger stakeholder populations.

Companies that encourage diverse talent by significant action and system changes are demonstrating their dedication to fostering an environment where equal chances are valued. Businesses that support the success of their neurodiverse employees will stand out as desirable employers to other people.

In fact, according to recent data, 72% of people said DEI had a key role in their decision to stay at a company.

This culture transformation can be great for everyone, according to Niamh Graham, SVP of Global HX at workplace solutions provider Workhuman, if it's genuine.

"To create an inclusive culture, organisations should first focus on fostering the kind of psychological safety that enables all employees to bring their whole, authentic selves to work—including feeling comfortable enough to bring up any issues with colleagues and managers without fear of retaliation."
Kate Griggs is the charity's founder and CEO. The founder of Dyslexia and author of This is Dyslexia believes that a neuro-inclusive workplace's culture is its key component.

Because it defines neurodiverse individuals by what they can do, rather than what they can't, cultivating a "skills-first" culture is crucial.

preparing the ground for victory

A neuro-inclusive policy is not without its challenges. Neurodiverse individuals may want additional job accommodations, such as noise-cancelling headphones, as well as the capacity to showcase their advantages in ways that don't penalise them.

Adam Boddison, a professor, is the CEO of the Association for Project Management (APM). He believes it's crucial to view neurodiversity as "brain variations" that can enhance project outcomes rather than as "brain deficiencies" to be avoided. He exhorts everyone to integrate practical inclusion strategies into daily tasks, such as converting to standing desks, encouraging regular breaks for mobility, and giving low-stimulation workstations away from the usual office hubbub.

Remember that even little adjustments can have a big impact on an organisation's ability to retain neurodiverse personnel. Kate Griggs suggests giving dyslexics extra time to read documents before meetings, providing big-picture summaries, and presenting material in a multi-sensory way in addition to using assistive technology where appropriate (using videos, graphics, diagrams, and less text).

Morcovcr, adopting a ncuro-inclusion strategy necessitates letting people with neurodiverse backgrounds deviate from established protocols and processes and doing away with the presumption of conformance to inefficient work methods.

L&D adaptations for neurodivergent thinking

When it is recognized that the difficulty lies with the organisation and not the individual, learning and development can be more effective.

Genius Within, an organisation that helps neurodiverse employees discover their skills while appreciating and accepting diversity, is managed by CEO Jacqui Wallis. The group offers policy advice to governments, consults with companies of all kinds, and oversees the Celebrating Neurodiversity Awards.

"Maybe the first obstacle is awareness. According to a report by the Westminster AchieveAbility Commission, we are aware that employers are not particularly aware of or understand neurodivergence. We also know that many individuals with neurodiversity are not aware of their strengths. Systemic change is removing all obstacles to outstanding performance by minimising all handicapping factors, including sensory and physical ones.

While there is so much area to cover, spreading awareness might seem like a tiny goal, yet it is an essential step towards neuro-inclusion.

Prof. Adam Boddison: "Ignorance is one of the biggest obstacles to achieving DE&I goals." Businesses don't actively choose to restrict workplace diversity, but misunderstandings and a lack of knowledge can have unforeseen consequences.

The added benefit of highlighting employees' positive contributions is that it helps the entire workforce.

It's crucial to keep in mind that variety inside an organisation brings value, not just one individual's viewpoint, he continues. It has been said that "enterprise methods that embrace neurodiversity are also those that are most likely to exemplify those business strategies that benefit all personnel."

Managers claim that the initiatives are already paying off in ways that go far beyond reputational enhancement, even though they are still in their infancy. SAP's program, which has been running for the longest among major corporations, is only four years old. They include boosting employee engagement levels and increasing productivity, quality, and innovative skills. No other project in his company, according to Nick Wilson, managing director of HPE South Pacific, which has one of the largest such programs, offers advantages on so many levels.

The most unexpected effect may be that managers have started to seriously consider how to best utilise all employees' talents by being more considerate of individual needs. According to Silvio Bessa, senior vice president of digital business services at SAP, the software "forces you to get to know the person better, so you know how to manage them." I'd without a doubt be a better manager as a result of it.

Why Possibilities Are Presented by Neurodiversity

According to John Elder Robison, a scholar in residence and co-chair of the Neurodiversity Working Group at the College of William & Mary, "Neurodiversity is the belief that neurological variations like autism and ADHD are the product of normal, natural variation in the human genome." "Many persons who embrace the concept of neurodiversity feel that people with differences do not need to be cured; they need aid and accommodation instead," adds Robison, who has Asperger's syndrome. Without a doubt, we concur.

We are all born differently and are raised differently, therefore everyone is to some extent differently abled (a term that many neurodiverse people prefer). Our thought processes are a combination of the "machinery" we were born with and the events that "programmed" us.

The majority of managers are aware of the benefits that diverse personnel backgrounds, disciplinary histories, gender, cultural origins, and other personal characteristics may bring to a business. Neurodiversity has similar, but more immediate, advantages. A company's efforts to produce or recognize value may benefit from the unique views that neurodiverse people can offer because they are wired differently from "neurotypical" people. Software testers at HPE who are neurodiverse noticed that one client's projects always tended to enter crisis mode just before a launch. They vehemently questioned the company's apparent embrace of the disarray since they were intolerant of disorder. This made the client organisation realise that it had grown too tolerant of these crises, and with the testers' assistance, the launch procedure was effectively redesigned. Thousands of SAP customers used the materials he generated after a neurodiverse customer-support analyst saw an opportunity to allow consumers to assist in solving a common problem themselves.

The neurodiverse population is still largely underutilised as a talent pool, nevertheless. The unemployment rate can reach 80%. (this figure includes people with more-severe disorders, who are not candidates for neurodiversity programs). Even highly competent neurodiverse individuals are frequently underemployed when they are working. Participants in the program told us tale after story about how they had to settle for professions that many people leave behind after high school, despite having strong degrees. People with master's degrees in electrical engineering, biostatistics, economic statistics, and anthropology, as well as bachelor's degrees in computer science, applied and computational mathematics, electrical engineering, and engineering physics, were among the applicants when SAP launched its Autism at Work program. Some had two degrees. Many have received honours or other distinctions for graduating with high honours and very high grades. One was a patent holder.

It should come as no surprise that many autistic individuals with these kinds of qualifications prove to be capable, and some are quite outstanding, whenever they do manage to get recruited. More than 30 participants in HPE's program have been hired for software-testing positions at Australia's Department of Human Services during the previous two years (DHS). The organisation's neurodiverse testing teams appear to be 30% more productive than the others, according to preliminary findings.

The Australian Defense Department is currently collaborating with HPE to create a neurodiversity program in cybersecurity. Participants will use their exceptional pattern-detection skills to perform jobs like searching logs and other chaotic data sources for indications of intrusion or attack. The Israeli Defense Forces (IDF) assessment techniques were used to identify applicants with "off the charts" relevant abilities. (The IDF's Special Intelligence Unit 9900 has a section staffed primarily with individuals on the autistic spectrum that is in charge of evaluating aerial and satellite imagery. It has demonstrated their ability to recognize patterns that others do not.)

With the growing skill shortages in technology and other areas, the case for neurodiverse employment is particularly strong. For instance, a study by the European Commission estimates that there would be an 800,000-person IT job shortfall in the European Union by 2020. The most significant shortfalls are anticipated in strategically significant and quickly developing fields like data analytics and IT services implementation, where jobs are well suited to the talents of some neurodiverse persons.

Why Businesses Don't Employ Neurodiverse Personnel

What has prevented so many businesses from hiring individuals with the skills they so desperately need? It all depends on how they identify and hire talent and select employees (and promote).

HR procedures are created with a focus on widespread organisation-wide implementation, particularly in large businesses. Scalability, however, conflicts intending to hire neurodiverse personnel. According to Anka Wittenberg, the company's chief diversity and inclusion officer, "SAP concentrates on having scalable HR processes; but, if we were to utilise the same processes for everyone, we might miss persons with autism."

Additionally, many neurodiverse individuals don't exhibit the traits that are typically associated with successful employees, such as effective communication, teamwork, emotional intelligence, persuasiveness, salesperson-like personalities, networking skills, and the capacity to follow rules without the need for special accommodations. These standards effectively eliminate neurodiverse persons.

Yet, they are not the sole means of adding value. Many businesses now place greater importance on their ability to compete through innovation. Companies that want to innovate must diversify their workforces, bringing in individuals and viewpoints from "the margins," as SAP described it in the press release announcing its initiative. Being surrounded by individuals who have diverse perspectives and may not fit in perfectly "helps offset our tendency, as a large firm, to all look in the same direction," according to Bessa. You would believe that businesses might continue to use their conventional hiring, developing, and recruiting methods while merely seeking a wider range of potential personnel. The strategy has been adopted by many: Its managers continue to work top-down, translating organisational positions, job descriptions, and recruiting checklists from strategies to the competencies required. But they miss out on neurodiverse talent due to two significant issues.

The first involves interviewing, a procedure that practically everyone performs when using the conventional strategy. Neurodiverse individuals may be exceptional in critical areas, yet many struggle in interviews. For instance, autistic individuals frequently avoid eye contact, are prone to verbal digressions, and are sometimes extremely forthright about their shortcomings. Some people struggle with confidence because of setbacks they encountered in prior interviews. In general, neurodiverse applicants are unlikely to perform better in interviews than less skilled neurotypical candidates. Thankfully, we'll discover that there are other methods besides interviews for determining a candidate's appropriateness.

The second issue arises from the presumption that scalable operations necessitate strict adherence to established methods. This issue is particularly prevalent in large corporations. As previously indicated, employees in neurodiversity programs often need to be given the freedom to stray from conventional wisdom. Creativity requires businesses to bring in individuals and concepts "from the fringes."

To share his company's expertise with others and convince multinational corporations to launch neurodiversity programs, Sonne founded the Specialist People Foundation (recently renamed the Specialisterne Foundation) in 2008. He did this because he was dissatisfied with the rate at which his own company could create jobs. The majority of those businesses collaborated with the foundation to implement some variation of the Specialisterne strategy. It comprises seven key components:

Join forces with "social partners" who have the knowledge you lack.

Managers in, let's say, a computer business is quite knowledgeable about a wide range of topics, but they are typically not specialists in autism or other forms of neurodiversity. Also, businesses are hesitant to intervene in their employees' private life, where neurodiverse persons might require additional support, for a variety of valid reasons.

The businesses we looked at formed partnerships with "social partners"—public or nonprofit institutions dedicated to assisting people with disabilities find employment—to close these gaps. Although HPE has worked with AutismSA, SAP has collaborated with the California Department of Rehabilitation, Pennsylvania's Office of Vocational Rehabilitation, the US nonprofits EXPANDability and the Arc, as well as international organisations like EnAble India (South Australia). Such organisations assist employers in navigating local laws governing the hiring of people with disabilities, recommend candidates from lists of neurodiverse job seekers, help with prescreening, arrange public funding for training, and occasionally carry out training. They also offer the mentoring and ongoing support (especially outside of work hours) necessary to guarantee the success of neurodiverse employees. In Germany, state funding for positions supporting the retention of neurodiverse employees has resulted from the realisation of the advantages of shifting people off public assistance and into occupations that generate taxable income. Estimates of the benefits a government receives from converting these individuals into tax-paying tech employees range, but they frequently are in the neighbourhood of $50,000 per person per year.

Use unconventional, non-interview-based teaching and assessment methods.

During the project-based evaluation period, candidates frequently exhibit complex collaborative and support behaviours despite the social challenges that many neurodiverse people face. For instance, divisions at HPE were tasked with creating a dependable robotic pill-dispensing system. One contestant froze throughout the presentation of the solutions. He said, "I'm sorry, I can't do it." "In my thoughts, the words are jumbled up." He was able to complete it because his neurodiverse teammates surrounded and reassured him as they sprang to his aid.

Such approaches extend the testing period to give candidates' abilities time to emerge. Of course, there are alternatives to this. HPE has started employing internships with comparable components.

instructing managers and other employees.

Quick, informal training sessions—some are only half a day long—help current employees learn what to anticipate from their new coworkers, such as the possibility that they may require accommodations and appear different. Managers receive slightly more thorough training to acquaint them with the resources available to help program participants.

Provide a supportive environment.

Simple support systems are created and maintained by businesses with neurodiverse programs for their new hires. One "support circle" is for the job, while the other is for an employee's personal life, according to

SAP." The person in charge of a group of program participants make up the workplace support circle. Employees that work on the same team as you as buddies can help you with everyday tasks, workload management, and prioritising. An "HR business partner," a work mentor, and a job coach are in charge of a group of program participants. Employees that work on the same team as you as buddies can help you with everyday tasks, workload management, and prioritising. Coaches for job and life skills are typically employed by social partner groups. Personal counsellors and counsellors for vocational rehabilitation are other types of social partners. Families of employees typically offer assistance as well.

HPE follows a different methodology. It groups new neurodiverse employees in "pods" of around 15 people, where they collaborate with neurotypical coworkers in a ratio of about 4:1 and are entrusted with addressing challenges linked to neurodiversity by two managers and a consultant.

HPE follows a different methodology. It groups new neurodiverse employees in "pods" of around 15 people, where they collaborate with neurotypical coworkers in a ratio of about 4:1 and are entrusted with addressing challenges linked to neurodiversity by two managers and a consultant.

Customise your career management strategies.

Much like other professionals, those hired through these programs require long-term career trajectories. This necessitates thoughtful consideration of continuing assessment and development that will take into account the unique circumstances of neurodiverse employment. Fortunately, over time, managers frequently develop a solid understanding of the skills and limitations of program participants. Participants go through the same performance reviews as other employees, but managers set objectives within those processes. No accommodations are provided for subpar performance, even though some goals may be related to participants' conditions. If anything, neurodiverse individuals have more obligations to meet because they must also meet program goals in addition to the performance standards that apply to all employees in their position. Some individuals exhibit the capability to quickly integrate into the organisation's mainstream and advance their careers. The purpose of HPE's pods is to offer individuals a secure setting where they may develop the skills necessary to work well and eventually move on to more mainstream employment.

In industries that neurodiversity programs affect, employee engagement has increased.

Extend the program.

By 2020, SAP plans to have 1% of its workforce that is neurodiverse. This figure was picked since it nearly reflects the prevalence of autism in the general community. Although they have refrained from setting specific numbers as goals, Microsoft, HPE, and other companies are all seeking to expand their programs. It's simplest to increase employment in industries like cybersecurity, business analytics, and software testing because these jobs are well-suited for neurodiverse people.

Nonetheless, SAP has assigned its over 100 program staff members to 18 positions. According to one boss, "The initial idea, as I understood it, was that these colleagues would primarily be focused on repetitive labour, such as software testing." Yet, in actual use, they have demonstrated their value in a considerably wider range of jobs. These include product management, which entails organising the creation of new SAP offerings; HR service associates; planning and organising HR activities; associate consultant; assisting clients in using SAP solutions to solve business problems; and customer support, which entails assisting clients over the phone in using SAP software. The last two disprove the notion that individuals with autism cannot work in positions requiring social skills.

Nine neurodiverse specialists are being sent out to client organisations at a time in pods, thus HPE is essentially selling packages of the cutting-edge skills resulting from neurodiversity. Because numerous people are put at once and because client demand broadens the range of feasible placements, the concept provides exciting scalability possibilities.

Promote the program broadly.

The popularity of neurodiversity initiatives has made several businesses consider how standard HR procedures might be excluding top talent. SAP is reviewing the best way to approach hiring, developing, and recruiting from a wider perspective. Its stated intention is to close its neurodiversity initiative by making its mainstream talent processes "neurodiversity friendly." Microsoft aspires to the same things.

Neurodiversity programs have a very wide range of advantages for businesses. Some examples are clear-cut: In hard-to-fill skill categories, businesses are now more successful at locating and hiring good and even great people. Lower failure rates and better production have benefited goods, services, and bottom lines. Both SAP and HPE cite instances of neurodiverse staff members working on teams that developed substantial inventions (one at SAP contributed to the development of a technical patch that saved the company an estimated $40 million).

Other advantages are more subtle. To accommodate for the challenges autistic employees have in understanding sarcasm and other finer elements of language, one CEO informed us that attempts to make corporate communications more straightforward have improved communication in general. Client organisations have improved their game and stopped considering some typical problems as inevitabilities as a result of some HPE software-testing pods' fastidious tendencies. Also, in the areas that the programs affect, employee engagement has increased: Areas the programs affect have seen an increase in neurotypical engagement: Those with neurotypical traits claim that being involved makes their work more relevant and raises their morale. Also, early results indicate that program participants are very loyal and have low turnover rates since they value the opportunity they have been given.

Not least of all, the programs offer reputational advantages. The businesses that invented them have received accolades for their global corporate citizenship and have been recognized by the UN as models of responsible management.

Managing a Neurodiverse Workforce challenge

Companies implementing neurodiversity programs have undoubtedly run with difficulties. Despite a large number of possible candidates, many of them are difficult to detect since universities do not categorise students according to their neurodiversity, and potential candidates do not always self-identify.

In response, HPE is supporting non-traditional "work experience" programs at colleges and high schools for neurodiverse students. They entail playing video games, programming robots, and other things. Microsoft is also collaborating with universities to enhance techniques for locating and utilising neurodiverse talent.

The broken dreams of applicants who are not selected for placement represent another frequent challenge and require delicate handling. In one company, the parents of a kid who was not hired wrote to the CEO because they were understandably sad. After all, the program had boosted their hopes that he would finally find meaningful employment. Management worried about a possible PR issue. The matter was eventually resolved through sympathetic conversations between the parents and program managers—some of whom had families that had gone through comparable difficulties.

Fairness and social norms-related issues could also come up. In one instance, we saw four workers in a neighbouring department crammed into a small area, causing complaints, but a program member with overstimulation issues was given his own office. After an explanation, those diminished. We have heard of occasions where autistic people's characteristic candour ruffled feathers. One raised questions when a program worker told a coworker, "You stink at your job." Such issues can be addressed with coaching from supervisors and mentors.

Some managers claimed that the program resulted in more work for them. For instance, some participants' perfectionist tendencies made it challenging for those employees to determine which flaws were worth repairing, which ones weren't, and which ones necessitated seeking out more guidance.

Another difficulty is dealing with the stress that neurodiverse workers experience. According to studies, participants had exceptionally high levels of anxiety as a result of unforeseen and unpredictable events, such as system failures that disrupted daily activities. Many of the persons we spoke with underlined the need of being understanding of program employees' stress. Some people simply work part-time to keep everything under control, which can be problematic, especially when deadlines are approaching. Organisations must have personnel who can identify problems early and take action before they get more serious to tackle these circumstances. Several managers claimed that with these and other supports, they could carry out their duties in a largely typical manner. In addition, SAP management discovered that contrary to their initial expectations, they could even supervise program participants remotely as long as local pals and mentors offered assistance.

Significant Changes in People Management

Companies and their leaders are encouraged by neurodiversity initiatives to adopt a management philosophy that emphasises placing each employee in a situation that would optimise their contributions.

SAP employs a metaphor to spread this concept throughout the company: Humans are like randomly shaped puzzle pieces. Because it's simpler to group people together if they are all perfect rectangles, businesses have traditionally pushed employees to cut away any flaws. But to do that, workers must leave their differences at home—differences that businesses require to innovate.

This implies that businesses need to adopt a different mentality, one that requires managers to do the difficult work of putting odd puzzle pieces together—to see people as unique individual assets rather than as receptacles for fungible human resources. Managers will have to work harder. The benefits for businesses, though, will be significant: having access to more of their employees' abilities as well as a variety of viewpoints that could help them compete more successfully.

Chapter 8

Living with Autism Spectrum Disorder and Creating an Autistic Life

According to the Diagnostic and Statistical Manual of Mental Disorders, autism spectrum disorder (ASD) is an example of neurodivergence. Autism is a sign of variations in the wiring and operation of the brain.

While many autistic individuals experience disabilities, some do not. Comparing those with autism to those who are deemed neurotypical, autism does not suggest deficiencies. Instead, it implies that a person may require various degrees of assistance and modification to flourish.

Sometimes receiving a diagnosis can feel daunting. It's critical to understand that autism is not a disease that requires treatment. It implies that a person may require various supports, environment modifications, and coping mechanisms to live complete lives with the fewest possible interruptions to their everyday functioning.

Autism is a neurological abnormality that manifests differently in every person but is characterised by several features. Some autistic people need routine and environmental modifications to function properly.

The emotional, physical, and social effects that autistic persons experience are examined in this article. It also offers advice to those looking after an autistic individual.

Strategies for Coping Emotionally With Autism

According to research, people with autism frequently experience anxiety and tension, which can negatively impact their ability to cope with stress and maintain their emotional well-being.

1.Some of these pressures are a result of societal expectations, which frequently demand that individuals with neurodiversity comply with neurotypical norms. In addition, compared to non-autistic people, autistic people are more likely to experience trauma and abuse.

2.Autistic children develop into autistic adults, even though autism features frequently first appear in early childhood. As a person gets older, their autism does not go away.

It can be challenging for an adult with autism to receive a diagnosis after living their entire lives without knowing why they are the way they are. Adults are often not evaluated by providers, and during evaluations, many autistic people receive incorrect diagnoses or are incorrectly informed they are not autistic. Individuals who can obtain an assessment from a competent provider can find it difficult to pay for the service.
Several members of the autistic community have accepted self-diagnosis as a result of these obstacles.
3.Self-diagnosis occurs when a person learns about autism and how autistic traits appear through research and discovers that this fits with their experience, but before being assessed or given a diagnosis by a provider.
A person who learns they are autistic later in life may experience a wide range of emotions in response to this knowledge, whether they

self-identified as having the condition or were given a diagnosis following an evaluation. As individuals evaluate earlier events in light of this understanding, they could be overcome with grief about not learning sooner or suffering overload. When individuals learn to uncover and live authentically outside of neurotypical standards of conduct, they could also spend a lot of time understanding their identity in light of this information.

4.Be aware of the emotional difficulties

A person's brain functions differently than what is regarded as neurotypical when they have autism, which is a type of neurodivergence. But because neurodivergent persons are frequently required to think, behave, and feel in neurotypical ways, they constantly feel under pressure to pretend to be neurotypical or present in that way.

Since many autistic people have at least one mental health diagnosis, these emotional responses may frequently mirror other mental health illnesses such as sadness, anxiety, and

PTSD. ADHD, seizures, sleep difficulties, and gastrointestinal disorders are a few more illnesses that might co-occur with autism.

5.For autistic people who are not allowed to learn how to process and express emotions in a way that comes naturally to them, dealing with the emotions associated with receiving an autism diagnosis is much more challenging.

How to Control Anxiety

Many autistic individuals struggle with anxiety. According to a 2019 study, 20% of autistic individuals reported having anxiety symptoms, compared to 9% of the control group.

6.Issues with daily life could be the cause of such worry. In addition, a lot of autistic people worry about social situations. People with autism often communicate differently from persons without autism, and they may have trouble understanding nonverbal social cues or the conventions of neurotypical social interaction. As a result of breaking these guidelines, they risk being called "rude." They could develop a fear of making errors or being misunderstood.

If you're having anxious symptoms, talk to your healthcare practitioner about management and symptom-relieving options, such as counselling.

Another cause of anxiety is sensing that others don't understand you. Communication difficulties, especially for those who are nonspeakers, might exacerbate anxious feelings.

A weighted blanket, doing art, taking a stroll, using a fidget toy, or doing breathing exercises are some relaxation techniques that may help manage anxiety.

People with autism are more likely to self-medicate for mental health issues.

7.Maintaining Health for Individuals with Autism

Every time an autistic person has a visit, medical professionals could concentrate on the person's autism diagnosis, which could lead them to miss other symptoms. Yet, it's crucial to maintain regular dental and physical examinations as well as yearly physicals. You can bring a supporter with you to these appointments, such as a spouse, relative, or friend, to assist you in speaking up for yourself and interacting with healthcare professionals.

Moreover, the following tactics can support maintaining physical health:

Self-care: It's crucial to engage in self-care activities including regular exercise, relaxing breaks, and stress management. Tasks, activities, and programs that suit your sensory requirements and level of energy may also be taken into consideration.

observing a regular schedule: Finding a technique to maintain a routine might be beneficial when it's possible since for autistic people, routine disruptions can occasionally be challenging. Regular sleep and waking hours, fixed mealtimes, daily self-care activities, and domestic duties can all be incorporated into a daily routine to help you keep a consistent schedule.

providing for an autistic person
Active Way of Life

There are numerous therapy options available to assist autistic individuals in managing their co-occurring diagnoses or meeting their support needs, but relatively few of these options incorporate a regular exercise schedule. Some autistic individuals may experience difficulties with their motor abilities, such as balance or walking. Dyspraxia and hypermobility are two examples of connected diagnoses.

According to research, keeping physically active can benefit autistic children's conduct, self-regulation, and communication.

7.Finding activities you enjoy will help you keep active and maintain good health if you have autism. Concentrating on things you want to do and that make you feel good while you're doing them might be beneficial for your physical and mental health.

Always Eating Balanced

Due to difficulties with food textures, odours, and other senses, some autistic people have a difficult time eating a healthy diet. Due to sensory sensitivities, many people have unique dietary requirements.

8.Finding foods that a person enjoys and that satisfy their nutritional demands may require some effort, but it's crucial to identify strategies for getting around these dietary preferences.

Be prepared to try (and likely reject) a variety of foods until you find any that you like, as this may require some patience and trial and error. It's crucial to be aware of the prevalence of eating disorders like ARFID and disordered eating in autistic people.

Using supplements, such as green powders, may be crucial or even required.

You can create a food schedule based on the foods you or a loved one enjoy and dislike by keeping a food diary.

Issues with Sleep

A lot of autistic people have trouble falling asleep.

9.Many factors,such as restlessness or overstimulation, might cause this. Adhering to a set bedtime routine will be helpful for you if you have autism and struggle to get enough sleep. Maintain a sleep journal and write the nights you have trouble falling asleep as well as any potential causes.

Social Effects of Autism Humans are relational creatures, and everyone requires some kind of social support. However, for a variety of reasons, autistic persons can occasionally have trouble with this.

Relationship building and maintenance can be challenging for some people due to communication problems and overstimulation.

Another big issue for those with autism is stigma. According to research, stigma against autistic people makes neurotypical people less likely to interact with them.

10.Even if there could be difficulties, someone with autism must receive enough social support. Family, friends, and local support group gatherings in their area might provide them with social support.

A support group for other autistic persons might help you connect with others in your local area if you have autism. A support group can assist you in managing your stress and providing the best care possible for your loved one who has autism. You get to interact with people who have faced comparable difficulties and experiences.

Giving and Aiding Others

It's crucial to keep in mind that self-care is equally as important whether you are caring for an autistic individual. Your loved one may need varied degrees of help and support, depending on their needs. Taking care of your mental and physical well-being enables you to give the autistic person you are caring for the best support possible.

A permanent type of neurodivergence is autism. Helping a person identify their strengths and learn strategies for coping with the difficulties that a neurotypical world frequently brings should be the main goal.

Increasing awareness of the needs and lived experiences of neurodiverse persons has been facilitated by self-advocacy, where traditional therapeutic techniques have generally centred on a normative agenda. Caregiving for an autistic person should concentrate on meeting the individual's needs, assisting them in communicating in a way that is efficient and comfortable for them, and treating any comorbid conditions rather than trying to "fix" the autistic person or teach them to behave in neurotypical ways and hide their autistic traits.

Most contemporary interventions concentrate on modifying settings to enhance functioning and applying techniques that optimise autonomy and well-being. Some autistic people have mentioned the value of coping mechanisms based on normal developmental processes.

Language-First Identity

Some occasionally can prefer to refer to someone with autism as a "person with autism." The phrase "autistic person," which puts identification first, is preferred by a large portion of the autistic community. By paying attention to and supporting the experiences of those with autism, you may support them and lessen stigma.

How to build an environment that is autism-friendly has been a question that more individuals have been asking themselves over the past several years. Families have remodelled rooms to create satisfying sensory experiences, and architects have written about developing autistic-friendly structures.

People with autistic spectrum disorders can view the world

extremely differently from other individuals, as is evident simply by listening to them. Something can be both empowering and incapacitating. We must work to lessen the negative consequences of sensory impairments and increase their positive benefits while designing an atmosphere that is welcoming to people with autism.

As each person on the autism spectrum will see the environment differently from a sensory perspective, the suggestions below are fairly general and should, whenever possible, be taken into account.

There are several questions we should be asking ourselves before we start remodelling a space or designing a structure to assist and guide how we will go about making adjustments that would be beneficial for people with autism. Several of these inquiries require an evaluation of the current environment, consideration of the seven sense markers, and attention to the users of the environment.

It's crucial to keep this in mind when analysing the questions regarding the senses because individuals with autism can either be hypersensitive (get excessive sensory information) or hypersensitive (receive too little sensory information). They may also be both hyper- and hypersensitive, requiring different amounts of stimulation at different times.

While attempting to create an environment that is welcoming to people with autism, we should consider the following:

•ability to see (Sight)
•audio perception (Hearing)
•Sense of touch and pressure
•odorant sense (Smell)
•sensation of taste
•hearing sense (Balance)
•kinaesthetic sense (Space)

questions involving visual information

How is the natural and artificial lighting in the rooms?
What shade do the walls have?
How many items in the space would need to be seen or recognized visually?
Do the furnishings, rugs, and drapes have patterns?

Many autistic people's sensory experiences are greatly influenced by lighting. Because some people can see the lights flickering at a rate of 60 flashes per second, fluorescent lighting can be distracting to the point of becoming incapacitating for them (60Hz). The flicker rate of some fluorescent lights is 120 Hz.

Natural daylight is important, particularly for sleep habits. Melatonin, a hormone that aids in regulating sleep/wake cycles, is one explanation. Melatonin often increases at night and decreases during the day. Making sure there is darkness when sleeping is one of several measures to attempt if persons with autism are having sleep issues.

It's crucial to pay attention to colour as well. We are affected differently by various colours. Red, for instance, has the longest wavelength and might energise us by increasing our heart rate. Yellow can excite and has a long wavelength. Bright blues have calming effects on the psyche and improve focus. Green can help you unwind. Do you want to create a dynamic environment or a relaxing one in the room you are designing?

The degree of clutter or minimalism in the spaces should also be taken into account. Many autistic individuals are especially attentive to every detail and can become overloaded with too much visual information. Some require greater stimulus from images.

Some people with autism spectrum disorders may find pattern-heavy clothing very upsetting. Patterns can be overbearing, disorienting, and even distort vision.

inquiries involving auditory input

Exist regular outside noises like traffic, kids playing, or construction?

Exist internal sounds on a regular basis, such as music, refrigerators buzzing, and clocks ticking?

Is it possible to lessen the amount of outside noise that enters the building?

Exists a way to individually reduce noise, such as earplugs?

Numerous individuals with autism have reported to us that they have a very high threshold for sound. The strength of noises they can hear can be deafening, and they can hear sounds that are much further away. They can hear a conversation in the room next door while blasting loud rock music in their headphones.

Issues involving pressure and touch

Is there a place where you can feel or stroke various textures?

Exist objects that can provide the skin with a variety of sensations, like sand or water?

Exist tools to apply pressure when necessary, such as wooden massagers? Some autistic individuals avoid touching unless they have control over it. Others require more pressure to feel secure and at ease, and when utilised properly, objects like weighted blankets can help. Some individuals who are very hypersensitive require further stimulus to experience (filter out too much sensory information as opposed to too little).

questions pertaining to smell (Olfactory)

Are there any odours from the outside that seep inside the building or into the room through the walls, windows, or doors?

Are there any odours from within the house that could be upsetting, such as those of foods, cleaning supplies, or perfumed goods?

Some autistic individuals find odours to be so overpowering that they feel quite nauseous. Even after the product has been taken out of the room or cupboard, some people will still smell it.

questions pertaining to flavour

It is important to keep in mind that sometimes we can presume a dislike for a flavour when the dislike could be for something else when designing a setting where the sense of taste will be engaged, such as dining rooms. Distaste may result from a reaction to the food's texture or look that causes discomfort. Questions to consider asking are:

It might be challenging for autistic people to understand their place in the physical world. Their feeling of identity can be developed by rocking, swinging, and balancing. If they need something directly behind them or in front of them to feel like themselves, having too much space in any direction can make them anxious. In addition, some autistic individuals get anxious if they can't see what's going on or where sounds are originating from because they find this to be extremely disorienting.

Many autistic individuals require space around them and are overwhelmed by commotion or clutter. They need to know there is a quick exit because they can feel caged in by the passageways.

Even though it might seem silly to ask, it's crucial to consider your options before responding. Adults or children may require a distinct setting. You might also need to think about whether a group with very different sensory needs will be using the same setting, or if other people who potentially have sensory variances will. Is there anywhere else a person can go to avoid the overload if there is a chance of sensory overload?

A Setting That Is Autism-friendly

What purpose will the room serve?

Certain areas, like school halls or open-plan offices, are used for huge gatherings of people. Some areas are designated for lone users or little groups. Yet, some areas, like corridors or lifts, are designed for transition.

People with autism spectrum disorders may find it challenging to shift from one area or activity to another, making transition spaces challenging.

Hence, it is important to think about how to make transition spaces simpler to navigate. You can inquire about things like -

Is it possible to move naturally between spaces without using a hallway? Are there any less confining methods of climbing or descending a building than using elevators?

Exist any smaller rooms that could be used for a retreat if necessary if the venues are being used for large groups of people?

Are there ways to seamlessly transition to a more open setting if the venues are tiny and intimate?

Can you draw a map of where people with autism seem to be anxious the most? Do any other options exist?

Conclusion

Architects like Maria Luigia Assirelli Dott. Arch (Rome) ARB, a partner in GA Architects, and Magda Mostafa, an associate professor at the Department of Construction and Architectural Engineering in Egypt, specialise in creating buildings that are autism-friendly. But, by taking into account sensory differences and the need for structure, we can all contribute to creating an environment that is welcoming to people with autism.

There are certain broad questions we may ask ourselves to establish a physical setting that will lessen rather than increase anxiety, even if every autistic person will have their particular environmental demands. All seven senses—visual, auditory, olfactory, taste, touch, vestibular, and proprioceptive—need to be considered. Space and its utilisation must also be taken into consideration.

It will never be easy to cater to everyone's preferences, but for some, a little thought and consideration can go a long way.

A Parent's Guide to Autism Treatment and Help

How to Help Your Autism Child Succeed

There are several ways you may help a child with autism spectrum disorder (ASD) get over their obstacles. These parenting-related suggestions, therapies, and services could be useful.

A Parent's Guide to Autism Treatment and Help

If you recently learned that your child may have an autism spectrum condition, you definitely worry and wonder what will happen next. Since no parent is ever ready to learn that their child is anything other than happy and healthy, receiving an ASD diagnosis can be extremely distressing. You could be confused by contrasting therapy ideas or unsure of how to help your child the most effectively. Also, if you've been told that ASD is an incurable, lifelong illness, you might be worried that nothing you do will make a difference.

Although it is true that ASD is not something one simply "grows out of," there are a number of treatments that can help children learn new skills and get beyond a variety of developmental challenges. Support is available, including free government assistance, in-home behavioural treatment, and school-based programs, to meet your child's unique requirements and enable them to learn, develop, and thrive in life.

It's essential to take care of oneself while caring for an autistic child. Being emotionally strong enables you to give your child the best care possible. The stress of raising a child with autism may be lessened by using these parenting tips.

Tip1:Stop holding out for an explanation.

Starting therapy as soon as feasible is the finest thing you can do as a parent of a child with ASD or related developmental delays. Get help as soon as you think there might be an issue. Don't wait to act in hopes that your child may catch up or outgrow the problem. It is pointless to wait for an official diagnosis. The earlier children with autism spectrum condition receive treatment, the better their chances of success. Early intervention is the most effective way to hasten a child's development and reduce autism symptoms over time. The better informed you are about conditions on the autism spectrum, the better decisions you can make for your child. Ask questions, educate yourself on the various treatments, and participate in making your own treatment decisions.

Develop knowledge in your youngster

. Learn what makes your child's challenging or disruptive behaviours stop and what causes them. What worries or frightens your child? Calming? Uncomfortable? Enjoyable? Knowing how your child is affected can enable you to address problems more skillfully and avoid or change difficult circumstances.

Cherish the peculiarities in your child

Instead of concentrating on how your autistic child is different from other kids and what he or she is "missing," try practising acceptance. Recognize your child's individual qualities, celebrate small accomplishments, and avoid putting your child in comparison to other children. More than anything, your child will gain from feeling accepted and unwaveringly loved.

Never surrender.

It is impossible to foretell how the autism spectrum disorder will develop. Never make any assumptions regarding the course of your child's life. Like everyone else, those with autism have a lifetime to develop and perfect their abilities.

Give structure and safety for your autistic child as the first piece of advice.

Your participation in their care and your attempts to learn as much as you can about autism will be extremely beneficial to your child. You'll both live more comfortably at home if you take the following advice:

Be trustworthy.

Children with ASD find it difficult to apply what they learn in one setting, such as a school or therapist's office, to another, such as their home. For instance, your child may use sign language at home to communicate with you but not at school. The best way to encourage learning is to provide your child's environment some consistency. Use the same techniques that the therapists are using with your child at home after learning about them. Consider having your child receive treatment in more than one location to aid in helping him or her transfer what they have learnt from one environment to another. Consistency is key when talking to your child and dealing with challenging behaviours.

Observe a schedule.
Children with autism frequently perform better when they adhere to a strict schedule or regimen. This is related to the constancy they both need and want once more. Make sure that your child has a schedule for meals, therapy appointments, school hours, and bedtime. Make an effort to minimise the frequency of interruptions to this procedure.

Prepare your child in advance if a schedule adjustment is unavoidable.

Reward positive behaviour. Try to "catch them doing something good" since positive reinforcement with children with ASD can go a long way. When you compliment them for good behaviour or when they learn a new skill, be very clear about the behaviour you are thanking them for. Think of other ways to praise them for good behaviour, including letting them play with a favourite toy or giving them a sticker.

Make your house a secure environment. Provide your child a private space in your home where they may relax, feel safe, and feel at home. This necessitates structuring and setting boundaries in a way that your child can understand. Visual cues could be helpful (coloured tape marking areas that are off limits, labelling items in the house with pictures). Also, if your child has a history of tantrums or other self-harming behaviours, you might want to safety-proof your home.

Tip 2: Learn nonverbal communication techniques.

Even though it can be challenging, you don't have to speak to or even touch an autistic child in order to establish a connection with them. You can communicate with your child by your voice tone, body language, how you look at them, and occasionally even how you touch them. Your child is talking to you even if they never speak. You only need to learn the language.

Pay attention to any nonverbal cues.

If you pay attention and pay attention, you can learn to spot the nonverbal cues that autistic kids use to communicate. You can tell whether someone is tired, hungry, or in need of anything by the sounds, the expressions on their faces, and the behaviours they take.

Find out what triggered the tantrum.

It's only natural to feel depressed when misunderstood or ignored, and children with ASD are no exception. According to research, children with ASD commonly act out when you miss their nonverbal signs. They use temper tantrums to get your attention and to convey their unhappiness.

See Autism Behavior Issues.

Schedule an enjoyable time. Despite having ASD, a child is still a child. Decide when your child will be most awake and alert for fun. Consider the things that make your child laugh, smile, and come out of her/his shell as you try to come up with methods to have fun together. If these activities don't seem therapeutic or instructional, your youngster is most likely to enjoy them. Both you and your child will gain a lot by taking pleasure in one another's presence and spending time together unhurriedly. All children need to play to learn, and it shouldn't feel like work.

Keep an eye out for your child's sensory needs.

Many kids with ASD have extreme sensitivity to touch, sound, light, smell, and taste. Analyse your child's "bad" or disruptive behaviours to see what sights, sounds, smells, movements, and tactile sensations they are drawn to, as well as what makes them feel good. What causes stress in your child? Calming? Uncomfortable? Enjoyable? You'll be more adept at solving issues, averting sticky situations, and fostering positive experiences if you know what impacts your child.

Tip3:Develop a specialised autism treatment strategy

It might be difficult to decide which treatment is best for your child when there are so many options available. You can receive various or even contradicting advice from your parents, professors, and doctors, further complicating the situation.

Remember that no single treatment is effective for everyone when creating a treatment plan for your child. Every autistic individual is different, with their own unique talents and shortcomings.

The course of treatment for your child should be personalised for their particular need. It is up to you to see that their needs are satisfied because you are the one who knows your child the best. You can achieve it by posing the following inquiries to yourself:

What are the strengths and weaknesses of my child?

What actions are the most problematic? What critical abilities does my child lack?

Which type of learning is best for my child: watching, listening, or doing?

What activities does my child want to perform, and how may those be used to help with treatment and to support learning?

Finally, remember that your participation is essential to the success of any treatment strategy, regardless of the one chosen. By collaborating with the treatment team and completing the therapy at home, you can ensure that your kid gets the most out of their treatment.

•Build on your child's interests in a good therapy strategy.

•Provide a foreseeable schedule.

•Teach tasks in small, manageable increments.

•Engage your child's interest directly in activities that are quite structured.

•Provide behaviour reinforcement on a regular basis.

•Participate the parents.
•selecting autism therapies
Behavioural therapy, speech-language therapy, physical therapy, occupational therapy, and nutritional therapy are just a few of the various treatments and methods used to treat ASD.

It's doubtful that you'll be able to treat all of your child's issues at once, even while you're not required to restrict your child to just one treatment at a time. Instead, begin by concentrating on your child's urgent needs and most severe symptoms.

Autism Interventions, Therapies, and Treatments

Tip 4:Search for help and help

Caring for a kid with mental imbalance can be time and exertion consuming, times when you feel cortisol, deterred, or overburdened.

Bringing up a kid with extraordinary necessities is much harder than nurturing a common young person. It's pivotal that you care for yourself to be the best parent you can be.

Don't attempt to handle everything by yourself. You're not required to! Families of children with ASD have a variety of resources at their disposal for guidance, assistance, advocacy, and support:

ASD support groups - Attending an ASD support group is a terrific opportunity to connect with other families going through similar struggles. Parents can rely on one another for emotional support, information sharing, and advice. The isolation many parents face after learning their child has a diagnosis can often be much diminished by simply being around others who are in the same situation and listening to their stories.

Every parent requires a break from time to time. This is especially true for parents dealing with the additional stress caused by ASD. Respite care allows you to take a break for a few hours, days, or even weeks by temporarily replacing you with another caregiver.

Refer to respite care.

Individual, marital, or family counselling - You may wish to see a therapist on your own if stress, anxiety, or depression are starting to affect you. Counselling is a secure setting where you can openly discuss all of your feelings, good, terrible, and ugly. Marital and family counselling can also assist you in resolving issues that the difficulties of raising an autistic kid are producing in your marriage or with other family members.

Free government services for autistic kids in the United States

The Individuals with Disabilities Education Act (IDEA), a federal statute in the United States, entitles children with disabilities—including those with ASD—to a variety of free or low-cost services. These services include medical assessments, psychiatric therapies, speech therapy, physical therapy, parent counselling and training, assisted technology devices, and other specialised services that are available to underprivileged children and their families.

For free services under IDEA, children under the age of 10 do not require an autism diagnosis. They are immediately eligible for early intervention and special education programs if they have a developmental delay, which includes delays in communication or social development.

services for early intervention (birth through age two)

The Early Intervention program offers support to young children up to the age of two. Your child must first go through a free evaluation in order to be eligible. You will collaborate with early intervention therapy professionals to create an individualised family service plan if the assessment identifies a developmental issue (IFSP). Your child's requirements and the exact services he or she will receive are detailed in an IFSP.

An IFSP for autism would incorporate various play, physical, speech, and behaviour therapy. It would concentrate on getting autistic children ready for the eventual switch to school. Early intervention services are often provided at a daycare facility or in the client's home.

Ask your paediatrician for a recommendation or use the tools given in the "Get more help" section at the conclusion of the article to find nearby early intervention options for your kid.

services for special education (age three and older)

Assistance is provided to children over three through school-based initiatives. Special education programs are adapted to your child's unique requirements, just as early intervention. Kids with autism are put in small groups with other kids who have developmental delays so that they can receive more individualised care and specialised training. Yet they might also spend at least some of the school day in a conventional classroom, depending on their skills. The idea is to put children in the "least restrictive environment" they can be in while still learning.

Your local school system must first assess your child if you want to pursue special education services. . It also outlines the unique services or supports that the school will give your kid in order to achieve those objectives.

know the rights of your child

You have the following legal rights as the parent of a kid with ASD:

•Participate in the entire IEP process for your child.

•Get your youngster evaluated by a third party.

•You can ask anyone you wish to be a part of the IEP team, from a family to your child's doctor.

•If you think your child's needs are not being fulfilled, you can request an IEP meeting at any time.

•If you can't reach a compromise with the school, you can get free or inexpensive legal representation.

•Taking care of a child with autism while having autism

According to research, autism has a genetic component. But many parents don't learn they have autism until after they do their research and get a formal diagnosis for their own child. If you have autism, raising children who are also neurodivergent may present special difficulties for you. The following advice could be helpful:

Don't conceal who you are. Allow your youngster to see who you really are. Do not feel under any obligation to hide any peculiar behaviours or bodily movements from your child if you have them. By being authentic, you give your autistic child permission to be authentic around you and provide the two of you a chance to connect over shared interests. Moreover, you can discuss with your child how neurotypical others could respond to your activities and how to handle unfavourable responses. Try to provide advice that you may have benefited from when you were younger.

Always take good care of yourself. If you suffer with sensory needs or need a highly regimented lifestyle, caring for a child can be difficult. A crying infant, for instance, may be a persistent source of stress and discomfort if you're sensitive to sounds. You may find it challenging to maintain a regular routine due to a child's unplanned tantrums, which will only make you more frustrated. It's crucial that you develop coping mechanisms that can help you feel less stressed in these kinds of circumstances in order to safeguard your own feeling of wellbeing.

Look for assistance from others if some jobs seem too difficult to handle. For instance, a parenting mentor or other parents of children with autism may be able to help you come up with solutions if talking with physicians and teachers is difficult.

accentuate your advantages. Everyone possesses unique strengths, and you are no different. Think about how your abilities can assist you in creating a nurturing environment for your child. Do you have a talent for design or visual thinking? For your child, create instructive posters. Can you maintain sustained concentration? Use that focus to learn more about parenting techniques and coping mechanisms. Are you adept at resolving issues? To solve problems around the house, use your imagination and innovative thinking.

Both you and your child deserve your patience. Recognize that you both have a lot of room to develop and learn. There could be some setbacks. You may lose your anger and feel embarrassed by your behaviour. Or perhaps your child struggles to fit in with their classmates when they first start school. Make a decision to learn from mistakes and find answers, even if it takes a few tries. Remember to recognize progress when one of you does it. Praise your youngster and acknowledge your own accomplishments as well.

Every person must endure challenges, hurdles, and difficulties throughout their life. Resilience is the capacity to endure hardship and overcome it. In order to develop confidence and competence in overcoming problems, resilience entails proactively navigating challenges. Being able to do so promotes mental health, and personal development, and enhances positive self-worth and self-esteem.

Because once a person has successfully handled a difficult event, they will feel more secure in their capacity to handle hard situations, resilience is a self-replicating trait. Resilience increases along with confidence.

People with autism often experience difficulties with their sense of confidence and worth. It can be overwhelming and terrifying to live in a non-autistic world. The absence of accommodations can cause tension, worry, and exhaustion. Successfully communicating one's requirements can be challenging, especially if the necessary supports are not in place. Unpredictability can make things stressful; novel activities can cause shutdowns or meltdowns.

Without resilience, autistic persons may find life more difficult, be unable to adapt to new conditions or changes, and may feel the need to isolate themselves from others. Early resilience development can give a child the self-assurance they need to take on new difficulties and succeed.

What advantages does resilience have?

An autistic person benefits from resilience:

•create self-confidence and self-esteem, as well as a strong sense of self as they navigate life's milestones.

•control alterations or unpredictability
•overcoming obstacles or disappointments
•lessens tension and worry
•conquering obstacles, accepting errors and mistakes, and learning from them.
•setting the stage for more autonomous adulthood by realising the value of practice in learning a new skill
•Fostering a sense of location and belonging requires an understanding of social-emotional boundaries and limits.
•develop your courage to take on new challenges
between childhood, adolescence, and adulthood

What prevents resilience from occurring?

Resilience development can be hampered or impeded by a number of factors, including:

When another person invalidates a person's identity, self, safety, experience, or beliefs, this is referred to as invalidation. Bullying, abuse, violence, or discrimination are all ways that this can take place. Instead of saying "You're learning how to" or "I'm learning how to teach you," saying "You can't" is invalidating. Building someone's confidence and reassuring them is both crucial for establishing a trusting connection.

Assuming Incompetence: This is something that frequently happens to autistic persons and can take many different forms, such as presuming they are incapable of making decisions, living independently, working, or maintaining friendships or relationships. Autistic people can lose their confidence and capacity to do things on their own if they assume they are incompetent, which can lead to negative and harmful self-fulfilling prophecies.

Overprotection - Parents or those who provide care and assistance may feel compelled to shield autistic individuals from obstacles or challenges. A person may begin to doubt their capacity to accomplish tasks if they are constantly shielded. Resilience is hampered by self-doubt.

Negative messaging - Rather than being defined by their abilities, autistic people are instead labelled by their weaknesses. Instead of being informed what they can do, they are told what they cannot. Developing resilience is tough when such a message is used.

Failures in the past - This can serve as both a tool for learning and a barrier to developing resilience. Resilience may suffer if mistakes are highlighted and concentrated on by adult role models or other significant figures in a person's life. Failure-related negative reactions might be traumatising or lead to ruminative thinking. Failure must be seen as a normal part of life, and assistance must be given so that people can move on and try again.

Resilience will be supported by a nonjudgmental discussion of failure and how to use the lessons learned in a similar circumstance.

Perfectionism can cause anxiety because it makes people strive for perfection and fear failing at a particular task. Because they are afraid their efforts won't be good enough, they may decide not to do the activity or, if they do, stop before finishing it. It's common to misinterpret the need for perfection with avoidance or difficult behaviour.

How can we increase resilience?

The key to developing resilience in practice. The best method to accomplish this is by introducing a series of controlled obstacles, and then gradually increasing those challenges. Consider it similar to sports training: move gently while introducing new workouts to raise the difficulty. When a youngster succeeds at one obstacle, the ideal scenario is that this would increase their strength and confidence to take on the next challenge. Parents find it particularly difficult to watch their kids struggle with tasks, but if we step in every time, our kids won't learn and develop.

I'll use my own two autistic children, who are now adults, as an example of a controlled challenge. I had Marc and Julia work with me in a farmer's market that my adult figure skating group owned and ran when they were 13 and 11 years old. The volunteers were somewhat predictable because my kids were familiar with all of them from our time together at the ice rink. Little activities were assigned to them, and when they mastered those duties, more were gradually added. They were also given clear guidelines on the working environment, such as the requirement to wear uniforms, the prohibition on using electronic devices while at work, and the fact that the market manager, not I, would be the one to give them orders.

They gained more confidence in a variety of areas during their nine years of employment at the market. They learned how to report to a manager, take instructions from a variety of people, and my son's diet expanded from less than 10 foods to eat every day (this was a phobia at the time they started volunteering). They also learned how to earn points every shift that they could redeem for things they wanted (the more expensive the item, the more points required so they learned that one has to work more hours for a pricier item). Marc was proud of and comfortable eating food that originated from his place of employment. That then developed into a horticulture course where he learned to grow his own fruits and vegetables in a garden. As a result, he began eating soup and salads at age 21, which is something I never imagined would happen.

Although these risks were highly supported, Marc and Julia were encouraged to try new things in the market. By offering support, anxiety levels were kept under control, and any errors made were treated as lessons. The skills they developed while volunteering in a safe, stress-free setting at the market helped them in future job experiences, which they were able to handle more easily.

Important Ideas to Teach Children About Resilience

The main ideas to convey to kids about resilience are:

Simply because something seems difficult doesn't mean you shouldn't attempt it.

You can get through obstacles if you get some assistance.

Nobody ever learns a talent off the bat; practice is necessary. Don't give up just because mastering a talent requires practice.

While trying something new, it's OK to seek a parent or another trustworthy person for assistance.

You'll feel great after overcoming a challenge, and you'll be able to attempt it again in the future with probably less difficulty.

It's acceptable to compete, and it's acceptable if you lose.

It's okay if you don't get it right the first time.

Early self-esteem and confidence development will operate as powerful safeguards for long-term well-being.

Also, they serve as the cornerstones of independence and resilience, both of which are essential for successful adulthood.

Conclusion

For proper social functioning, people with autism spectrum disorder (ASC) struggle to integrate emotional responses into their decision-making and exhibit cognitive biases. Hence, gaining insight into the fundamental causes of the changed decision-making in people with ASC may ultimately improve their social functioning. The Image Decision Task was used to study how confidence levels, interpretive context (verbal cues), and fresh information (fragments of an incomplete picture) affected decision-making. 49 children with ASC and 37 children with Normal Development completed the assignment in our study (TD). When an explanatory context was provided, success rates among children with TD increased. Conversely, whether or not an interpretative framework was given, children with ASC had an identical chance of success. Also, in contrast to children with TD, the level of confidence did not permit forecasting the likelihood that judgments made by children with ASC would be effective. Third, children with ASC were more likely to make snap judgments or decisions based solely on a small portion of the information available. In light of contemporary cognitive and affective theories on ASC, these findings are discussed.

A new theory of how relationships develop shunned psychoanalytic models and argued that social engagement occurred through other kinds of "social" engagement that, ironically, were actually being described at a more abstract level. Any child who was a solitary thinker and struggled to understand the mathematical and logical properties of the world was now on "the autistic spectrum," an anomaly within a new model of the development of relationships. Instead of drawing from the psychoanalytic theory of human relationships, these texts increasingly drew from cognitive models in order to describe how children became social subjects. Now that the new model of autism was accepted as the absence of social development, 'social development' in children also came to be redefined.

Along with these changes was the definition of autism changing. These were brand-new descriptions of the social environment that supported psychological growth, produced by epidemiologists and psychologists with training from the Institute of Psychiatry. This approach was especially open to the "autistic spectrum" psychology because it gave the child a new sense of agency. The days of adults forcing their theories of evolutionary development onto an infant's still-developing brain were long gone; today's infants had autonomy and the democratic capacity to change how they perceived themselves through statistical patterning. The psychology of society would be collected, documented, and examined if more kids avoided the psychologist's gaze, stared blankly at their inquiries, and played with their toys like they were scientific instruments. Because the people it represented were the most disadvantaged, this voice and this organisation reflected the psychology of the autism spectrum in its entirety.

It is because of this that a "social disability" became both a defect and a virtue.

The prospect that statistical, epidemiological, and genetic studies would one day be able to define the term "autism" resided at the core of autism's second metamorphosis. The promise of an "autistic" mind, according to dominant descriptions of autism, such as Baron-Cohen's, resides in its capacity to reason logically, scientifically, and quantitatively. This is not a coincidence, but rather a reflection of how epidemiological models have been constructed in order to evaluate the idea and assert the scientific validity of their conclusions. The second definition of autism was, in many respects, just a mirror of the tools that have been employed to measure, contain, classify, and label components of the developing mind that are simply unknowable. The way this inaccessible aspect of the infantile psyche has been communicated actually says a lot more about the society that created it than it does about the infantile mind itself. There will be new "styles of reasoning" regarding society, individuality, and the entitlement to have individual children's needs recognized if the tide shifts again and autism undergoes another metamorphosis. Whether these substantial gains have occurred for other reasons or whether children with autistic spectrum disorders have been misclassified in the past, the potential of autism to transform these various fields of human knowledge should not be ignored. Although they may benefit from many of the same educational strategies as kids with other developmental disabilities and share some of their characteristics, kids with autism spectrum disorders present special challenges for their families, teachers, and other caregivers. Even the teaching of basic facts is difficult due to their deficiencies in verbal and nonverbal communication. To draw and maintain their children's attention, the particular challenges in social interaction (such as in shared attention) may call for more individualised coaching than for other kids. However, regular peer interactions rarely happen without intentional planning and ongoing structure provided by the adults in the child's setting. Children's motivational systems and the interpretation of their experiences are impacted by the lack of typical friendships and peer interactions. One of the most challenging and crucial lessons a child with autism spectrum disease will have to learn is how to communicate appropriately with others. In addition, there is a significant prevalence of behavioural issues, such as temper tantrums, self-stimulatory behaviour, and aggressive behaviour. Many children with autism spectrum disorders, whose motivation or interests can be limited, require a systematic selection of rewards. This calls for creativity and ongoing effort from teachers and parents in order to maximise the child's potential. Although there are general learning and behaviour analysis principles that apply to autistic spectrum disorders, understanding the unique characteristics of the disorder should help analyse the contexts (such as communicative and social) of behaviours for specific children and lead to more effective programming. For instance, a functional assessment that takes into account circumstances can be conducted, and dysfunctional behaviours can subsequently be replaced with more appropriate communication techniques. Recommendations 1-1 Children with any autistic spectrum disorder (autistic disorder, Asperger's disorder, atypical autism, PDD-NOS, childhood disintegrative disorder), regardless of the level of severity or function, should be eligible for special educational services under the category of autistic spectrum disorders as opposed to other disabilities because of their shared continuities and their distinct social difficulties.

Any family that has a child with autism spectrum disorder faces difficulties. Families can be involved in the education of young children with autism spectrum disorders on a variety of levels, including advocacy and acting as educators and collaborators in the classroom. Change in behaviour as well as a family-centred approach that takes into account the needs and assets of the family as a whole. A parent component was present in almost all empirically supported treatments that the committee assessed, and the majority of research projects took a parent-training strategy. The advantages of a family-centred orientation or combined family-centred and formalised parent training in supporting parents require more research. Though little is known about the effects of cultural differences, such as race, ethnicity, and social class, nor about the interactions between family factors, child characteristics, and features of educational intervention, it is well established that parents can learn and successfully apply skills to changing the behaviour of their children with autistic spectrum disorders. Having a child with an autism spectrum disorder adds stress for the majority of families. Effective teaching strategies used by parents, as well as community and family support, can significantly reduce that stress. In order to fulfil their obligations, parents must have access to accurate information on autism spectrum diseases and the variety of available services and technologies. Also, they require timely information on evaluations, lesson plans, and resources that are accessible to their kids. They need to be informed in a way that provides them time to get ready to carry out their tasks and obligations. The media's focus on autism spectrum disorders and the Internet's ubiquitous accessibility have boosted parents' awareness over the past ten years, but they have also frequently presented viewpoints that are not balanced or well-supported scientifically. The issue of how to inform parents and ensure their active participation in advocating for their children's education is of utmost importance.Suggestions Planning for education should actively incorporate the issues and viewpoints of parents. In particular: a. The local school system should give the parents written information about the nature of autistic spectrum disorders and eligibility categories, the range of alternatives within best practices in the early education of autistic spectrum disorders, and sources of funding and support so that they can be effective members of the Individualised Education Plan (IEP) team that plans a child's education. b. The local school system should give each family the written results of their child's assessment before the IEP meeting.

www.ingramcontent.com/pod-product-compliance
Lightning Source LLC
Chambersburg PA
CBHW071057250726
48662CB00019B/1108